吴晟

Wu Sheng

My Village

SELECTED POEMS

吾鄉: 吳晟詩選

1972–2014

吳晟
Wu Sheng

TRANSLATED BY
John Balcom

ZEPHYR PRESS
BROOKLINE, MA

Cover image by Tân Gī-jîn (陳義仁)
Book design by *type*slowly

Zephyr Press, a non-profit arts and education 501(c)(3) organization,
publishes literary titles that foster a deeper understanding of cultures
and languages. Zephyr Press books are distributed to the trade in the U.S.
and Canada by Consortium Book Sales and Distribution [www.cbsd.com].

Zephyr Press acknowledges with gratitude the financial
support of the National Endowment for the Arts, the Massachusetts Cultural
Council and Mr. Tzu-hsien Tung, who supported the translation and
publication of this book.

Cataloguing-in publication data is available from the Library of Congress.

ISBN 978-1-938890-79-6

ZEPHYR PRESS
50 Kenwood Street
Brookline, MA 02446

www.zephyrpress.org

Contents

Footprints on the Heart   *John Balcom*

Farmer, poet, essayist, and environmental activist, Wu Sheng (吳晟) has mapped the social, economic, political, and environmental issues confronting his home, Taiwan, for the past forty years and more. He is a local writer who has gained considerable recognition at home for his committed support for the island's environment, usually at odds with Taiwan's expanding structures of neoliberal globalization.

Wu Sheng entered the literary scene in Taiwan when his nativist poems about his hometown began appearing in the early 1970s. They were far different from the dense, nearly incomprehensible aesthetic objects produced by Taiwan's fashionable modernist writers. Wu's poems were neither abstract nor difficult: no dazzling imagery, no difficult language, no urbanity, and no affected existential angst. Instead, Wu wrote about life in rural Taiwan—the sweat, toil, dirt, and boredom—the only existential drama he knew. And he wrote clearly and without romanticizing.

Wu Sheng, the penname of Wu Shengxiong (吳勝雄), was born in 1944, the fourth of seven children in a farming family. His father received some schooling and worked in the local Farmer's Association until his early death in 1965; his mother was illiterate and worked in the fields from a young age. During Wu's formative years, Taiwan was still predominately an agricultural society and, like many children of his day, he went to school in addition to working long hours on the family farm. Home for Wu Sheng is Chenliao village, located in the heart of the area straddling southern Changhua county and northern Yunlin county in west-central Taiwan, one of the island's prime agricultural regions. The rich, fertile soil produces a wide variety of crops including rice, sugarcane, and peanuts. Wu's home sits amid green fields in a landscape criss-crossed by streams and irrigation ditches, and watched over by mist-shrouded mountains.

Wu's surroundings, the events of his own life, and his family history have provided the raw materials for his poetry. Taken together, his poems are a vivid and personal account of Taiwan for four and a half decades, as it has passed through years of profound and sweeping socio-economic change. Upheaval and continuity are central concerns in his poems: What happens to an agricultural society that undergoes rapid modernization? What remains of traditional values after industrialization, urbanization, and economic and cultural integration through forms of globalization? Wu's poems are a local response.

Although Wu's writings consciously acknowledge that the way of life he honors is threatened, he continues to cling tenaciously to the traditions and values of rural Taiwan, while questioning and resisting the new. And just as Wu rejects modern urban values, which he sees as containing a lack of value, he has likewise rejected literary fashion: Modernism has come and gone; Postmodernism has arrived, and it undoubtedly will be supplanted by something else. Wu has remained stubbornly loyal to his nativist roots. He is not averse to moralizing. His texts are often pointedly didactic, an approach unfashionable in artistic circles, but one that continues a long literary tradition in China.

To put Wu's writing in perspective, it is essential to know something of the recent history of Taiwan and its literature. The political climate in the early 1950s tended to inhibit the growth of a strong literary scene, and poetry in Taiwan remained relatively undeveloped. The Nationalist KMT government was still jittery after the Communist victory on the Mainland; the beginning of the Korean conflict in 1950 and the fall of Hainan Island in 1951 did not help ease concerns. The political situation had intense cultural ramifications: much of the Mainland's recent literary heritage and the island's own nativist literature written in Japanese had been proscribed by the government as being potentially subversive. Government-supported anti-Communist literature had a strong presence in Taiwan. The only other poetic options at the time were the lyrical but innocuous sentimental verse made popular by writers from the 1930s like Xu Zhimo, or models provided by the various schools of modern Western writing.

In the late 1950s, a number of significant literary magazines began publishing. Writers whole-heartedly embraced Western-inspired Modernism as the only progressive choice for art in an era of propaganda. In addition to promoting their own versions of Modernism, these magazines introduced modern Western literature to their readers. Inspired by Western writers such as Kafka, Joyce, and Eliot, Taiwan's modernists wrote difficult and obscure works of fiction and poetry. Existentialism and Surrealism were all the rage. Many Taiwan-based writers, especially the Mainland emigres, discovered a peculiar resonance in these schools of writing with their own tragic situation. The difficulty and obscurity usually associated with modern Western art seemed ideal for expressing the uncertainties of the time. By the 1960s, Modernism had all but eclipsed ant-Communist poetry in Taiwan.

Wu himself began writing poetry during the heyday of Modernism in the early '60s. Interestingly, though Wu was an insatiable reader of modernist literature, it never had a profound or lasting influence on his own style. Wu attributes this to three factors. First, the modern poems he first encountered were all easy-to-understand lyric poems from the 1930s and '40s. Secondly, since he lived in the countryside and worked on a farm, he had a difficult time trying to understand the "loneliness" and "alienation" so common in modernist works, which were largely written by and for educated urbanites. Modernist writing did not conform to life as he knew it. Third, after Wu's father died tragically in an automobile accident in 1965, he was forced to face some very harsh realities with a determination and pragmatism well beyond his years. In 1966, he self-published his first collection of poetry titled *Tossed About*.

After college and a one-year stint working in Taipei, Wu returned home to stay. He and Zhang Fanghua, a college classmate, were married and the two of them lived in the traditional three-sided courtyard house with Wu's mother. During the day, he worked as a biology teacher in Hsichou Junior High School, and upon returning home he and his wife helped his mother in the family fields. At night he wrote. It was only after his return that Wu Sheng was able to find his true voice as a poet. It was as if he were able to tap into the spirit of the place, awakening all of his latent emotions. His poetic voice is intimately linked to his home—its light, climate, and geography—and it is his particular sense of place that provides it authority. As a poet, he speaks not only for his own village, but for all rural areas across the island. His poetry has validity because he is able to capture in words the specific changes that Taiwan was experiencing by focusing on the immediate and commonplace. At the same time, the archetypal simplicity of the situations he depicts allows him to transcend the strictly regional and to explore universal truths. By opting for nativism, or rather a regional response to modernity, Wu has intentionally placed himself outside of the literary mainstream.

His first truly significant work, a series of sixteen poems written between 1972 and 1974, *Impressions of My Village*, set the pattern for his poetry in coming years. His language is plain, simple, and colloquial, in stark contrast to the modernists of the day who were obsessed with developing highly individualistic styles often based on deliberate syntactic distortions of the Chinese language. His poems are sprinkled with the local dialect, providing them a greater sense of place.

Wu's poetry seemed to answer a basic human need for centeredness and meaning in the flux and chaos of existence. This is particularly true of those who lived through the radical economic and social changes of the 1960s, '70s and '80s. During those years the island's economy shifted from agriculture to an export-oriented economy with a significant percentage of the population moving to urban areas. The breakdown of rural society has been blamed for the breakdown of traditional values in Taiwan. Thus, Wu's return to the landscape and its human presence evoke a sense of permanence within the complete and utter breakdown of traditional human relations. Regional awareness, in Wu's poems, functions as an antidote for modernist and industrial disease.

While the lyric voice in each of the poems proclaims its allegiance to the old ways, there is an underlying awareness that it is a losing battle. Progress cannot be stopped; all resistance is ultimately doomed. The speaker in the poems is clearly a villager, but one who is able to stand outside himself and objectify his experience. This is significant because the "gap" between actual village life and the speaker's critical perception of it indicates a degree of alienation—values and traditions have broken down to the extent that the speaker is able to see himself apart from his surroundings and to comment on the situation from the point of view of someone who knows he is being pushed to the periphery.

Another feature of the series is the fatalist tone of some poems. The speaker often ends a poem with the observation that life for everyone leads to the same end. The perception is only magnified by the speaker as he frequently situates himself within the larger cyclical flow of time over the generations who bring forth their children to work the land and in the end to return to it. Yet there is a stubborn strength within this apparent pessimism. On one level I am reminded of Robert Frost's poem "The Gift Outright" in which he says: "The land was ours before we were the land's,/ She was our land more than a hundred years/ Before we were her people." For Wu Sheng, then, the villagers are the land: to respect the land is to respect oneself; to reject the land and its traditions is to reject one's own self.

Wu Sheng's poems from the early 1970s deal with rural life in a general way; they evoke a mood without addressing specifics. In the years following, his poems begin to take on greater thematic focus. The generalizations of his *Impressions* series gives way as Wu Sheng writes about his mother and father and specific aspects of the rural environment. Nearly a decade after his father died, enough time had elapsed for Wu Sheng to develop an emotional distance from the event, which allowed him to begin exploring his relationship with his father. Poems such as "Embankment," "Wheels," and "Ten Years" all deal with a common theme: the personal continuity of life and values. From father to son, generation after generation, a way of life and a set of values are passed on.

In the mid-'70s, Wu Sheng also began to focus on specific aspects of his environment in another series of poems dealing with plants commonly found in rural Taiwan. In each poem, Wu emphasizes a specific aspect of each plant—the betel palm, a sensitive plant— offering it a connotation symbolic of some characteristic of rural character or life, such as stamina or honesty. Most of the poems have a didactic purpose that can be read as moral homilies. During the same period, Wu Sheng also wrote a series of poems on various domestic animals. Some of his animal poems are also homiletic, while others depict traditional customs and beliefs, such as "Animal Spirit Tablet."

Wu Sheng continued writing poems about rural Taiwan even while it seemed to be disintegrating around him. During the 1970s, the demographic movement to urban areas continued apace with another ten percent of the population moving into urban centers. Economic prosperity remained the rule as wages shot up; fifty percent of the population was now considered middle class. Education was also on the rise with thirty-seven percent of the population completing secondary school as opposed to only nineteen percent in 1968. With a ninety-percent national literacy rate, popular culture was in great demand and through the medium of television, which nearly every household could afford, people were exposed to new ideas from abroad. While these advances were true for urban areas, rural areas lagged behind—farm wages, for example, were only about two-thirds that of non-farm wages. Young people were leaving the farm for a better life. As the urban standard of living improved, people scorned low-paying, back-breaking farm work, opting for easier, better-paying factory jobs and the promise of opportunity. The government utilised money and resources to make the urban industrial areas the productive center of Taiwan's economy, while the rural areas seemed to fall through the cracks of social and political concern.

The inroads of "progress" and the slowly crumbling resistance in rural areas tended to inject a defensive tone into Wu's poetry. From 1977 to 1983, he wrote a series of twenty-nine poems titled "Speaking to the Children." The speaker in these poems tends to be an authority figure—a teacher, father, or older brother—addressing his children, his students, or future generations. At the heart of these poems is the marginal relationship of the countryside to the urban center. The poems are concerned with the effects of modernity in the form of urban commercial culture on the countryside and traditional values. Wu

Sheng attempts to maintain the balance between message and medium. However the didactic tone of his work increases, perhaps due just as much to his work as a school teacher as to the socio-cultural climate. Poems in the series such as "Father Firmly Believes" and "Growing Up" are rhetorical and concerned with maintaining a sense of rural dignity in the face of an urban culture perceived as superior. The message behind all of these poems is that respect for the land is a form of self-respect.

In the late 1970s, Wu also wrote a series of poems called "Stupidly Honest Letters" critiquing the trend among gifted university students of going abroad to study, and the subsequent brain-drain to the United States. The poems all take the tone of letters from home; the speakers in the poems are all apparently farmers or workers attempting to understand why their talented friends and relatives have moved overseas and, in some cases, have become citizens of their adopted country. Poems such as "You Too Have Left" and "American Citizenship" are examples. The demographic process depicted in these poems reenacts that of an earlier day—first, young people forsook the countryside for the city, and now, the best and brightest are forsaking the island for a new country. The rural periphery has grown, and the entire island of Taiwan stands in a marginal relationship to the global center of the US.

The language of some of these poems is looser, more prosaic, seemingly less focused and more reproving in tone. The speakers of the poems complain about relatives or friends who have left the island and immigrated to the US. The accusatory tone captures the the feelings of betrayal felt by many of those who remained in Taiwan.

In September 1980, Wu Sheng accepted an invitation from the University of Iowa to take part in the International Writer's Program. He stayed in Iowa for four months. His visit resulted in a series of eight poems in the form of letters home to his wife, titled, naturally, "Letters from Iowa." Ironically, but not surprisingly, the speakers in the poems have all realized the dream of going abroad only to find that once they have arrived in the US they all want to return home. His poem "At the Breakfast Table" is representative of the series. Homesickness, the feeling of being cast adrift, predominates in the Iowa poems.

After returning to Taiwan, Wu Sheng found it difficult to write poetry. He turned to writing prose pieces instead and from 1985 to 1994 wrote scarcely any poetry. In an interview in 1994, Wu attributed his writer's block to the impact of going to the States. His poetic silence could also have been interpreted as a sign that he had given up his quixotic quest to roll back time. In Taiwan, a position such as that in Wu's poems was generally seen as a nostalgic yearning for an age that would never return. Nativism was no longer a form of local cultural resistance. Nativist nostalgia began to serve a different purpose. The past was appropriated for commercial use and devalued by an omnivorous commercial culture. The finer aspects of Taiwan's rural past were marketed as part of a mainstream commercial culture for selling everything from junk food to political candidates. It was difficult for regional writing to retain its significance.

During this period, the island's economy continued to prosper and the material quality of life improved. However, what was becoming apparent to Wu was that these improvements came with a price: the environment was being seriously degraded. After restrictions on the sale of farmland for non-agricultural purposes were lifted, rural areas were increasingly becoming threatened as land became the object of large-scale speculation. The exodus from rural areas only increased. In 1993, construction began on the Jiji Dam across the Zhuoshui River, the largest construction project of its sort undertaken by the KMT government. Heralded as a project to benefit the people, by the time the dam was completed in 2001, it produced dire consequences for those living along the river and the farmers who relied on the water and nourishing silt that the river delivered to Changhua fields. In fact, the dam was built to supply water for the petrochemical industry in Mai Liao. During this time, Wu became actively involved in political campaigning.

By 1994, Wu Sheng once again found his voice and inspiration in his rural surroundings, by speaking out about the environmental, social, and cultural crises that he saw. Over the next five years, he would write another series of poems entitled "Goodbye to My Village." His early poetry had dealt with the cultural ramifications of industrialization:

the destruction of local communities, the weakening of traditional values and social bonds, and the denigration of the rural. The poems in this new series focus on the widespread trend of land speculation, the degradation of rural areas, and environmental issues of public importance. There are also poems of nostalgia and a longing for the past, linking them closely with his early work *Impressions of My Village*. These poems were included in his *Selected Poems* published in 2000.

The arrival of the new millennium brought change. Wu and his wife retired from teaching, and it was time to undertake several projects Wu had long been contemplating. The first was to write a lyrical exploration of the Zhuoshui River. Wu secured a one-year position as a writer in residence for Nantou County, which would allow him to complete the Zhuoshui River book project. The second project was a long-cherished dream to reclaim land and plant a tree park. In the late '90s, Wu purchased land near the family farm and was able to secure a lowland reforestation grant to help fund the project.

The Zhuoshui River is the main artery running through Wu's homeland; it is also the longest river in Taiwan. The river's headwaters are deep in the mountains of Nantou County, fed by springs and tributaries that flow through Yunlin and Changhua counties. Wu had always dreamed of exploring the river from its headwaters to where it enters the sea. In 2001, Wu and his wife spent a year exploring the river. Wu had planned to write a lyrical account of their observations, but it was not to be. What Wu encountered was alarming: hyper-deforestation in the high-mountain headwaters, dams, and dredging had all horribly degraded the river.

In 2002, Wu published *A Notebook on the Zhuoshui River*, reissued in 2014 in the expanded edition *Protecting Mother's River: Diary of the Zhuoshui River*. The pure lyricism Wu had expected to inject into the work became more strident in tone. The book is a work of reportage with lyrical elements. The book clearly possesses a function of advocacy, with an interest in affecting social, political, and environmental change. It was clear that the people of Taiwan had little moral or affective relations with the river and Taiwan's environment.

Wu had also grown disillusioned with finding a political solution to the environmental problems, as he found that most government officials were working in collusion with the forces of development and progress.

It was also during this time that Wu began planting his tree park known as Purity Park (純園), named after his mother. Wu planted two hectares with mostly native species of trees including Michelia (Michelia compressa), camphor trees (Cinnamonum camphora), Japanese Zelkova (Zelkova serrata), Chinese pistache (Pistachia chinensis), Philippine ebony (Diospyros philippinensis), Taiwan incense cedar (Calocedrus formosana), indigenous cinnamon (Cinnamonum osmophloeum), and orange jessamine (Murraya panuculata). Wu claims that his motives for creating the tree park were to provide an outdoor space for families and a place where people could learn about and enjoy some of the native trees of Taiwan. On another level, it was no doubt an act of individual resistance to push back against the current of development and environmental degradation. A book titled *The Poet Who Planted Trees* provides a detailed account of Wu's activities.

In 2005, one of the most controversial projects to have been proposed in Taiwan was the Kuokuang Petrochemical Project. The original plan was jointly proposed by the CPC Corporation, forty-three percent of which was owned by the Taiwan government. The plan called for the construction of a petroleum refinery, naphtha-cracking plant, paraxylene plant, twenty-three midstream and downstream petrochemical plants, fourteen cogeneration units, and thirteen dedicated industrial piers on 2700 hectares of intertidal mudflat and natural wetlands at a cost of US$32.2 billion. The site chosen was the island's last significant intertidal mudflat and natural wetland, and home to a large variety of wildlife, including the Chinese white dolphin, a small and diminishing population of which is found on Taiwan's west coast.

When the plan came up for environmental impact review in 2009, permission seemed a foregone conclusion. However, in 2010,

Wu Sheng, as chairman of the Lai Ho Foundation, began to organize opposition. He knew the government was in bed with the industrial partners and that only grassroots opposition could make a difference. He called a press conference to announce the intention of the "the nation's artists to protect the mouth of the Zhuoshui River to ensure a healthy future for Taiwan." A broad range of highly visible activities—including concerts, debates, and demonstrations—increased public awareness of the project and the plight of the wetlands. A volume of documents associated with the protest *Wetlands, Petrochemicals, and Imagining an Island*, edited by Wu Sheng and the environmentalist and novelist Wu Mingyi, was published in 2011. Public opposition became so pronounced that the environmental impact process dragged on for over 600 days. Finally in 2011, President Ma Yingjou announced that the project was being abandoned.

However, victory was short-lived. Almost immediately, Wu and the island's activists were confronted by yet another river-capture project as part of the fourth phase of development of the Central Taiwan Science Park. Wu Sheng wrote, "We have reached a point where we must reassess our relationship with the land. Taiwan's industrial development has reached its limit or even surpassed it. The west coast is nearly dead and there is little land left uncontaminated. If the fourth phase deprives us of more water, it will mean the end of Changhua agriculture." Wu views agriculture from a long-term perspective; for him it is the foundation of the nation and grain is a form of national defense for which there is no economic value. He asks how a price can be put on air, water, and soil, the basics upon which human life depends. Eventually, mobilization resulted in the unfinished project being shut down.

Wu Sheng's work has become a cultural fixture of the island, with his poems and essays now anthologized in school textbooks. His poetry has also been set to music: *Sweet Burden*, a CD of poems and songs interpreted by various composers, was issued in 2008. This was followed in 2014 by *Picnic*, which contains Wu's poems set to music by his son Wu Zhining.

Wu Sheng and his wife still live in the family's traditional three-sided courtyard farmhouse. After Wu's mother died, his eldest son, a cardiologist, and his wife and children moved into the wing that had served as Wu's library. Three generations still reside in the old home. But Wu and his wife ended up having a modern glass and concrete "book house" built for Wu's collection of nearly ten thousand volumes. An avid reader, Wu began collecting books when he was very young. The collection contains many rare and early editions of modern literature, including copies of works once proscribed by the government that Wu had preserved, despite their criminality.

In 2014, he published his most recent collection of poetry *He Is Still Young*, which the poet confides might well be his last. The poems were all written from 2001–2014. Environmental protection and the health of the land are prominent themes, but there is also a new concern with the uncertainty of life. Poems such as "Loofa Arbor" deal with the issues of environmental protection and the disappearance of traditional culture. The poem refers to the traditional calendrical period of the beginning of autumn (立秋), a time on the island when the heat of summer would typically begin cooling. However, the continuing heat mentioned in the poem is part and parcel of global warming. The loofa arbor is a feature of traditional rural life that has nearly disappeared. People would often gather under a loofa trellis to cool off and perhaps seek entertainment by telling stories. All of this has disappeared as people live isolated lives inside air-conditioned homes watching TV. Obviously the degradation of the environment is intimately linked with the disappearance of local culture.

In the collection, the poet appears to view the world through the lens of his own mortality, writing poems on the passing of his mother, and a number of friends. Poems such as "Soda Pop," for example, are written in clear simple language, like the best of Wu's writing. He spends more time looking back over the past events of his life, but often with an anxious eye to the future, knowing that so much work remains to be done to ensure the future of his home, Taiwan.

Acknowledgments

I became acquainted with Wu Sheng's poems when I was a young student in Taiwan more than three decades ago. I was instantly attracted to the straightforward simplicity of his writing and his honesty as a poet; I also valued his poems for the insights they have provided into many of the island's local concerns. Wu Sheng, always a warm and enthusiastic friend, has been supportive of my efforts as a translator over the years, for which I thank him. Along the way, a number of people have read and commented on these translations: Howard Goldblatt, William Matheson, Nancy Ing, Chi Pang-yuan, and Michelle Yeh. I thank them all. The translations in this book were done over a period of nearly forty years. A number of them have previously appeared in print: I wish to thank *Upriver/Downriver*, *The Taipei Chinese PEN*, *Manoa*, and the *Taipei Review* as well as Columbia University Press for permission to reprint a number of poems from *Frontier Taiwan*, to University of Washington Press and Unitas for permission to reprint from *Sailing to Formosa*, to the National Academy for Research, Taipei, for permission to reprint poems from *Beyond the Music*, and to Taoran Press to reprint translations from a small chapbook, long out of print, *My Village*. Portions of the introduction appeared originally in an article written on Wu Sheng for the *Taipei Review* and I am pleased to be able to quote from it. I also wish to thank Christopher Mattison of Zephyr Press for his continuing editorial support.

Special acknowledgment is due to Mr. Tzu-hsien Tung for funding this translation and for his ongoing efforts to promote literature from Taiwan abroad. Most of all, I wish to express my heartfelt gratitude to my wife Yingtsih, also a translator, for her unending support and assistance over the years.

吾鄉

My Village

序説

古早古早的古早以前
吾鄉的人們
開始懂得向上仰望
吾鄉的天空
就是那一副無所謂的模樣
無所謂的陰著或藍著

古早古早的古早以前
自吾鄉左側綿延而近的山影
就是一大幅
陰鬱的潑墨畫
緊緊貼在吾鄉人們的臉上

古早古早的古早以前
世世代代的祖先，就在這片
長不出榮華富貴
長不出奇蹟的土地上
揮灑鹹鹹的汗水
繁衍認命的子孫

Preface

Long, long ago
The people of my village
Began to stare up with hope
The sky of my village
Is indifferent
Indifferently blue or gray

Long, long ago
My village lay in the mountain's shadow
A vast ink painting
Dark and troubled
Pasted on the faces of my people's village

Long, long ago
For generations on this piece of land
Where no wealth or prosperity grows
Where no miracles are produced
My ancestors wiped away their sweat
And brought forth their fated children

1972

路

自從城市的路，沿著電線桿——
（城市派出來的刺探）
一條一條伸進吾鄉
漫無顧忌的袒露豪華
吾鄉的路，逐漸有了光采

自從吾鄉的路，逐漸有了光采
機車匆匆的叫囂
逐漸陰黯了
吾鄉恬淡的月色與星光

自從吾鄉恬淡的月色與星光
逐漸陰黯
吾鄉人們閒散的步子
攏總押給小小的電視機

而路還是路
泥濘與否，荒涼與否
一步跨出，陷下多少坎坷
路還是路，仍然
——引向吾鄉的公墓

Roads

Since the roads from the city, lined with telephone poles
—Spies sent from the city—
Have encroached, one after the other, into the countryside
Unscrupulously offering luxuries
The rural roads have grown dazzling

Since the country roads have grown dazzling
The clamoring of machines
Has slowly blotted out the simple light
Of moon and stars in the countryside

Since the simple light of moon and stars
Has grown dim in the countryside
Leisurely strolls
Are mortgaged for television sets

But a road is still a road
Muddy or deserted
One step can lead to so much misfortune
A road is still a road, like always
Leading each to a common grave

1972

入夜之後

入夜之後，遠方城市的萬千燈火
便一一亮起
亮起萬千媚惑的姿態
寥落著吾鄉的少年家

入夜之後，收音機的流行小調
　（哭了幾千年還在哭的歌仔戲）
便在店仔頭咿咿唔唔
溫暖吾鄉老人家的淚腺

入夜之後，疲憊的路燈下
吾鄉囝仔郎捉迷藏、打陀螺的遊戲
以及村民未經潤飾的開講
喧鬧著吾鄉寂寞的夜晚

When Night Falls

When night falls, myriad lights switch on
One after another in the distant city
Bright with beauty and seductive charms
Filling the young men of my village with such loneliness

When night falls, a popular song can be heard on the radio
(A sad song from a folk opera sung for thousands of years)
At the country store
It brings tears to the eyes of the old folks in my village

When night falls, the kids of my village play hide-and-seek
And spin tops under weary street lights
The boys and girls chatter noisily
Brightening my village's cheerless night

1972

店仔頭

或是縱酒高歌，猜拳吆喝
或是默默對飲，輕嘆連連
或是講東講西，論人長短
消磨百般無奈的夜晚

這是我們的店仔頭
這是我們的傳播站
這是我們入夜之後
唯一的避難所
千百年來，永遠這樣熱鬧
永遠這樣荒涼

千百年來，千百年後
不可能輝煌的我們
只是一群影子，在店仔頭
模模糊糊的晃來晃去
不知道誰在擺佈

花生，再來一包
米酒，再來一杯
電視啊，汽車啊，城裡回來的少年啊
不必向我們展示遠方
豪華的傳聞

The Country Store

Whether playing drinking games, getting drunk
        and singing loudly,
Drinking quietly together and sighing
Or chanting and gossiping
We waste so many nights

This is our country store
This is where we come for news
This is the only place to go for amusement
After night falls
It's always this lively
—always this empty

For thousands of years and more to come
We, who will never amount to anything,
Are just a bunch of shadows
Moving hazily about the store
Not knowing who's pulling the strings

Have some more peanuts
Have another cup of rice wine
TVs, cars, young people back from the city
There's no need to tell us
All the fancy news from afar

店仔頭的木板橙上
盤膝開講，泥土般笨拙的我們
長長的一生，再怎麼走
也是店仔頭前面這幾條
短短的牛車路

Sitting cross-legged on store benches
Chewing the fat, clumsy hicks
Where else are we to go in this long life?
But down the short ox-cart road
In front of the store

1972

神廟

雖然，土地祠的荒蕪
已在吾鄉人們的心中
無盡蔓延
吾鄉的神廟
香火依然鼎盛

雖然，耶穌枯乾的雙手
曾捧來奶粉和洋大衣
畢竟不歸屬吾鄉
吾鄉的神廟
香火依然鼎盛

初一十五，或更重要的節日
吾鄉的人們必定在廟前擺上牲禮
燃一炷香、燒一疊金紙
祈求神祇保庇
吾鄉的人們，不能保庇自己

吾鄉的人們，從未懷疑
天公或大大小小的神祇
只知照顧自己

The Temple

Although the desolation of the Earth God's shrine
Occupies the hearts of my people's village
Spreading endlessly
The temple in my village
Is, as usual, filled with incense smoke

Although Jesus once offered
Dry milk and foreign overcoats with his withered hands
He never belonged to my village
The temple in my village
Is, as usual, filled with incense

On the first and fifteenth of the lunar New Year
        And on other important holidays
The people of my village
Bring offerings to the temple
Light a stick of incense, burn spirit money
Seeking blessings from the gods
The people of my village cannot look after themselves

The people of my village never doubt
The greater and lesser gods
They only know how to look out for themselves

1972

清明

年年清明節日
吾鄉的人們
必定攜帶祭品和銀紙，去墓仔埔
祭掃祖先的墳墓

祖先的顏面，識或不識
吾鄉的人們
祭拜時，悲傷或不悲傷
傳統的虔誠依然

吾鄉的人們，祭拜著祖先
總是清清楚楚地望見
每一座碑面上，清清楚楚地
刻著自己的名姓

年年清明節日
吾鄉的人們
必定去吾鄉的墓仔埔
祭拜自己

Tomb-sweeping Festival

Every year on the Tomb-sweeping Festival
The people of my village
Must take offerings and spirit money to the cemetery
And piously sweep the ancestral tombs

The faces of ancestors may no longer be remembered
And when the people of my village worship them
They may not be sad
But they maintain a traditional sincerity

When the people of my village worship ancestors
They always clearly see
Their own names carved
On every gravestone

Every year on the Tomb-sweeping Festival
The people of my village
Must visit the cemetery
To worship themselves

1972

陰天

似乎欲風而風兮不起
似乎欲雨而雨兮不來
仰長了脖子觀望天色的鵝群
兀立庭院，怔怔的納悶著

天色，始終是不風不雨
卻拉長了臉壓迫而至的天色
偶爾，一兩隻不耐煩的狗仔
繞著鵝群吠幾聲寂寞
鵝群的納悶依然
無情無緒去應和

仰長了脖子觀望天色的鵝群
觀望了一陣之後
結果，結果總是
一搖一擺、一搖一擺地
晃進和天色無關的籠子裡

Dark Skies

It seems like the wind is about to blow
        but it never does
It seems almost on the verge of raining
        but it never does
A goose stretches its neck
        to scan the sky
Standing motionless in the courtyard
        curiously ill at ease

In the sky, there is no sign of wind or rain
Just an oppressive sky
Occasionally a couple jittery dogs
Circle the goose and bark forlornly
The goose remains unperturbed
Responding without any emotion

The goose stretches its neck
        to scan the sky
After looking around for a while,
Waddles back to its pen
Which has nothing to do with the sky's moods

1972

雨季

抽抽煙吧
喝喝燒酒吧
伊娘——這款天氣

開講開講吧
逗逗別人家的查某人吧
伊娘——這款日子

發發牢騷罵罵人吧
盤算盤算工錢和物價吧
伊娘——這款人生

該來不來，不該來
偏偏下個沒完的雨
要怎麼嘩啦就怎麼嘩啦吧
伊娘——總是要活下去

Rainy Season

Have some smokes
Have summin' to drink
Damn this lousy weather

Shootin' the crap
Jokin' about someone else's wife
Damn this lousy day

Bitch and moan
Add up your wages and the cost
Damn this lousy life

When it's s'posed to rain it don't
When it ain't s'posed to
It rains not lettin' up
Does as it please
Pourin' down rain
Damn, just go on livin'

1972

晨景

雀鳥無關快樂不快樂的歌聲
還未醒來
吾鄉的婦女
已環坐古井邊
勤快地浣洗陳舊或不陳舊的流言

無關輝煌不輝煌的老太陽
還未爬上山頂
吾鄉的囝仔郎
已在母親的一再催喚下
悻悻然離開
沒有童話、沒有玩具的睡夢

吾鄉的老人，在屋簷下
細數瑣碎而黯淡的回憶
打發無關新鮮不新鮮的空氣
目送吾鄉的男人
牽著牛，踏上永無休止的另一種征途
昔日他們踏過的征途

哪！吾鄉的晨景
傳說是一幅美麗的圖畫

Morning Scene

The bird never considers
        if it's song is happy or sad
Not yet fully awake
The women of my village
Sit around the old well
Diligently washing the gossip, old and new

The old sun, never considering glory,
        has yet to climb over the mountains
The children of my village
After repeated orders from mothers
Have awakened from sleep
Without fairytales or toys

Under the eaves, the old people of my village
Go over the dull, broken fragments of memory
Killing time, not fresh or stale
They watch the men of my village
Harness the oxen and trudge off on another march
Just like they once did

Ah, this village scene
Is a beautiful painting
        or so the legend goes

1972

稻草

在乾燥的風中
一束一束稻草，瑟縮著
在被遺棄了的田野

午後，在不怎麼溫暖
也不是不溫暖的陽光中
吾鄉的老人，萎頓著
在破落的庭院

終於是一束稻草的
吾鄉的老人
誰還記得
也曾綠過葉、開過花、結過果

一束稻草的過程和終局
是吾鄉人人的年譜

Rice Straw

Sheaths of rice straw
Left in deserted fields
Tremble in a dry wind

Under a not so warm
Yet not so cold afternoon sun
The old people in my village wither
In crumbling courtyards

The old people in my village become
Sheaths of rice straw
Who remember
They once flourished, blossomed and bore grain

The life and fate of rice straw
Is the story of my village

1972

曬穀場

夏日，收割季
吾鄉的曬穀場
是一驚惶的競技場

氣象臺的報告
往往屬於謠傳
而天色，變幻不定的天色
吾鄉沒有諸葛亮之流的人物
可以預測

晴晴朗朗之際，誰也不知
太陽，何時將陰著臉
拂袖而去。天公
何時將遣來一陣
不爽快的細雨，或是一場
惡作劇的西北雨

吾鄉的曬穀場，在收割季
是一驚惶的競技場
時時，驚惶著吾鄉的人們

Grain Drying Yard

Summer, harvest season
The grain drying yard in my village
Is a competitive arena filled with dread

Weather reports
Belong to the realm of rumor
And the weather, the ever changeable weather
My village lacks someone of Zhu Geliang's caliber
To predict

When it's bright and clear, who knows
When the sun's face might darken
And go off in a huff. When will
Heaven dispatch an unpleasant drizzle or
A mischief-making northwestly rain

The drying yard in my village at harvest season
Is a form of competition filled with dread
Filling the people of my village with a near constant panic

1972

輓歌

──我生長的小村莊

是的，我曾體驗過年輕
年輕的飛翔
在我生長的小村莊
我曾體驗過年輕的徬徨
每一晚迷茫的星光都知道

是的，我曾體驗過春天
春天的芬芳
在我生長的小村莊
我曾體驗過春天的霉味
每一片腐爛的落花都知道

是的，我曾體驗過愛
愛的沉醉
在我生長的小村莊
我曾體驗過愛的絞痛
你每一道淒涼的凝視都知道

是的，我曾體驗過歌
歌的激盪
在我生長的小村莊
我曾隱隱聽見自己的輓歌
每一株墳場的小草都知道

Dirge

—the village where I grew up

Yes, I learned from my youth
I tested my wings
In the village where I grew up
I learned in my youthful uncertainty
As every dim star knows

Yes, I learned from spring
The fragrance of spring
In the village where I grew up
I learned from the spring mildew
As every decaying flower knows

Yes, I learned from love
The heady intoxication of love
In the village where I grew up
I learned of the painful bonds of love
As your every sad glance knows

Yes, I learned from song
The emotions in a song
In the village where I grew up
I heard my own faint dirge
As every blade of grass in the cemetery knows

1973

水稻

風雨怎樣凌遲
蟲害怎樣侵蝕
不可信靠的天空
怎樣以多變的臉色戲弄
吾鄉的人們

千年以來，吾鄉的人們
怎樣默默揮灑
費盡思量的汗水，滋潤你們
並以怎樣焦慮的深情
殷殷勤勤呵護你們

而你們無閒去思索、去議論
千年以來，一代又一代
你們的根，艱困的扎下土裡
你們的枝枝葉葉
安分的吸取陽光

當鐮刀和打穀機，開始
忙碌的合唱鳥仔在你們頭頂上
興奮的飛翔
只有你們明白
每一粒稻穀，是多少的辛酸結成

Rice

Though wind and rain kill slowly
Though insects eat too much
And the unpredictable sky
Toys with the people of my village
With its many moods

For a thousand years, the people of my village
Have wiped away their sweat in silence
Watering you with the sweat of exhaustion
They have looked after you
With so much loving anxiety

Too busy to think or discuss
Generation after generation for a thousand years
Your roots have bitterly penetrated the soil
Your stems and leaves
Have quietly absorbed sunlight

When scythes and threshers busily
Start to sing in unison
And the birds flutter
Over our heads
Only you know how much hardship
Has gone into each grain

1974

泥土

日日，從日出到日落
和泥土親密為伴的母親，這樣講——
水溝仔是我的洗澡間
香蕉園是我的便所
竹蔭下，是我午睡的眠床

沒有週末、沒有假日的母親
用一生的汗水，辛辛勤勤
灌溉泥土中的夢
在我家這片田地上
一季一季，種植了又種植

日日，從日出到日落
不知道疲倦的母親，這樣講——
清涼的風，是最好的電扇
稻田，是最好看的風景
水聲和鳥聲，是最好聽的歌

不在意遠方城市的文明
怎樣嘲笑，母親
在我家這片田地上
用一生的汗水，灌溉她的夢

Soil

Day after day, from sunrise to sunset
Mother, who lives near the soil, says:
The irrigation ditch is my bathroom
The banana orchard is my restroom
Under the bamboo is my noon nap's bed

She has no weekends or holidays
She has diligently watered
A soil-bound dream with a lifetime of sweat
Planting our family fields
Season after season

Day after day, sunrise to sunset
Mother, who knows no fatigue, says:
The cool breeze makes the best fan
The paddy fields make the best scenery
The birds and water make the best song

Without a care for how civilization in the distant city
May mock, Mother
Has watered her dreams for our land
With a lifetime of sweat

1974

浮木

然後，不經意間，又是夜了
又是黯淡的燈與燈
打著呵欠對視
一些年輕的激情
已是久遠久遠的事了

所有空空泛泛的聲音
在你更為空泛的凝視中
楞楞地懸掛著
一些些的蕭邦或杜布西
又能挽救什麼？

期期艾艾而去的歲月裡
我只是一塊浮木
任水流擺佈的一塊浮木
勞累中草草了結的一日
以及，漂流中
乏善可陳的所有往事
什麼也沒留下
只留下斑斑創痕
等待你的包紮和愛撫

這樣貼近又這樣遙遠的你
竟然坦開這樣無告的寂寞
向我索求依恃

Driftwood

And then, unawares, it's night again
Dim lights
Face one another and yawn
Youthful passions
From long ago

And then the hollow sounds
Are suspended in
Your even blanker gaze
What can Chopin or Debussy
Save

In the stammering passage of time
I'm a piece of driftwood
A piece of driftwood at the water's mercy
Hastily ends another day in exhaustion
And drifting about the water, there is
Nothing good to be said about the past
Nothing remains
Save the wounds that
Await your dressing and caress

Now at hand, now far away, you
Showed me your unspeakable loneliness
And asked me for support
But I'm just a piece of driftwood

我只是一塊浮木啊
任水流擺佈的一塊浮木
期期艾艾而去的歲月裡
隨著一個一個漩渦
逐漸在敗壞

A piece of driftwood at the water's mercy
In the stammering passage of time
Tossed about on one whirlpool and another
A toll is gradually taken

1974

土

赤膊，無關乎瀟灑
赤足，無關乎詩意
至於揮汗吟哦自己的吟哦
詠嘆自己的詠嘆
無關乎閒愁逸致，更無關乎
走進不走進歷史

一行一行笨拙的足印
沿著寬厚的田畝，也沿著祖先
滴不盡的汗漬
寫上誠誠懇懇的土地
不爭、不吵，沉默的等待

如果開一些花、結一些果
那是獻上怎樣的感激
如果冷冷漠漠的病蟲害
或是狂暴的風雨
蝕盡所有辛辛苦苦寫上去的足印
不悲、不怨，繼續走下去

不掛刀、不佩劍
也不談經論道說賢話聖
安安分分握鋤荷犁的行程
有一天，被迫停下來
也願躺成一大片
寬厚的土地

The Land

Bare-armed, who cares about the latest fashions?
Barefooted, who cares about being poetic?
Wiping away sweat you chant your poems
Intoning your own verse
Who cares about affected literary moods, much less
Becoming a part of history?

Lines of awkward footprints
Are written in the honest soil
Along the broad fields over which
Our ancestors sweat
Never contending, never arguing,
          silently waiting
If the flowers blossom and bear fruit
Who can ask for anything more?
If blistering blights
Or violent storms come
Erasing those bitter footprints
There is no sadness, no sorrow
          they will continue

No swords or knives are worn
There are no learned discussions on virtue and wisdom
Be content
Hoeing and plowing
For one day you'll be forced to stop
And lie down
A part of the broad earth

1975

輪

橫在我家門前，有一條馬路
馬路沿著小河流，以及兩旁的稻田
向西而行，通往街道
街道前端，是父親在那兒吃頭路的農會
農會斜對面，是父親
每月去匯款給我們的郵局
父親那一部舊腳踏車的輪子
便在這條馬路上
日復一日，年復一年，轉了又轉
直到那年年底，父親
在街道轉角處
被超速的卡車輾斃

橫在我家門前，有一條馬路
馬路沿著小河流，以及兩旁的稻田
向西而行，通往街道
街道前端、農會隔壁
是我在那兒教書的學校
學校斜對面，是我
每月去匯款給弟妹的郵局
我這一部新腳踏車的輪子刊
便在這條馬路上
日復一日，年復一年，轉了又轉
直到哪年哪天，我的新腳踏車
也會悄悄的舊吧
也會悄悄的消失吧

Wheels

A road runs in front of my house
Down along the stream, paddy fields on both sides
To the west it intersects a street
At the head of the street the farmer's co-op
      where father worked
Kitty-corner from the post office
Where father mailed us money each month
The wheels of my father's old bike
Rolled day after day, year after year
Along this road
To the end of the year, when
Turning that corner
He was hit by a truck

A road runs in front of my house
Down along the stream, paddy fields on both sides
To the west it intersects a street
At the head of the street the farmer's co-op
      where I work
Kitty-corner from the post office
Where I mail money to my brothers and sisters each month
The wheels of my new bike
Rolling day after day, year after year
Along this road
Until my new bike
Gradually gets old
Gradually wears out

1975

檳榔樹

投你們的影子，在我的影子
之上，投你們
寧靜、蕭穆、而且修長的影子
在我的仰望之中
在清晨、在日暮、在夜晚

你們是樸拙的母親撫養的
我也是；我們一起長大——
是親親密密的好兄弟
憨直的好兄弟

曾經，我離開你們
躲進重重典籍圍困的宮牆
如今，我歸來，靠近你們
你們仍可聞到
滿身的泥土味，和你們一樣

和你們一樣，我歸來
以盤錯交結的根，深深伸入
厚厚的土壤中
以疏疏朗朗的葉，朗朗舉向
遼闊的天空

Betel Palm

You cast your shadow over mine
You cast your serene and solemn shadow
Long and slender
Over my up-turned gaze
Dawn, dusk, or night

You were raised by a plain and simple mother
So was I, we grew up together
We are like brothers
Naïve and direct

I left you once
To hide among weighty books
            encircled by bitter walls
Cold and dark
But today, I return to walk among you
Perhaps you can still smell
The soil heavy on me, the same as you

Like you, I return
With tangled roots stretching deep into
The thick, rich soil
With plain leaves reaching for
A distant sky

投你們寧靜、肅穆、而且修長的
影子，在我的呼吸之中
在清晨、在日暮、在夜晚
我聞到你們
恬淡自如的清香

You cast your serene and solemn shadows
Long and slender
Over my breath
Dawn, dusk, or night
I smell your
Natural fragrance, the same as always

1975

牽牛花

在陽光下奔跑、在月光下嬉戲的
吾鄉的囝仔郎，哪裡去了
他們蹲在小小的電視機前面
吾鄉的牽牛花，不安的注視著

在陽光下流汗、在月光下歌唱的
吾鄉的少年郎，哪裡去了
他們湧去一家家的工廠
吾鄉的牽牛花，寂寞的尋找著

在陽光下微笑、在月光下說故事的
吾鄉的老人家，哪裡去了
他們擠在荒涼的公墓
吾鄉的牽牛花，憂鬱的懷念著

有一天，我們將去哪裡
吾鄉的牽牛花，惶恐的納悶著

Morning Glory

Where have all the children of my village gone?
Who once roamed under the sun
      and played beneath the moon
Now they sit in front of television sets
The morning glories in my village
      watch anxiously

Where have all the men of my village gone?
Who once toiled under the sun
      and sang beneath the moon
They've gone to the factories
The morning glories of my village
      search in loneliness

Where have all the old people in my village gone?
Who smiled under the sun
      and told stories beneath the moon
They've gathered in the desolate graveyard
The morning glories of my village
      think of them with sorrow

Where will we all go one day?
The morning glories of my village
      Wonder with apprehension

1975

十年

地球還是一樣的轉
不快也不慢
我的腳踏車的輪子
還是一樣的轉

沿着河岸，也沿着您
奔波了二十餘年的鄉間小徑
隨朝陽轉向辦公廳
再隨夕陽轉回家

留連不斷的水聲
沿途不由自主的潺潺
彷彿是，自您離去後
諄諄切切的叮嚀

說不上甘願或不甘願
來來去去的轉動中
路旁的稻穗，已不知黃熟了幾度
我已不是
耽於狂熱夢想的少年

父親啊，鄉人都說
我越來越像您
像您髮越稀，額越禿
像您容易為鄉人
牽掛和奔走
這就是您殷殷的寄望嗎

Ten Years

The earth keeps turning
Not fast or slow
The wheels of my bike
Turn the same as ever

On the path along the stream
You rushed around for more than twenty years
To work with the rising sun
And home again with the setting sun
The sound of flowing water never ceases
It flows without choice
As if your encouraging words
Have not stopped since you left

It's not a matter of being willing
In my comings and goings
I don't know how many ears of grain
       by the roadside have ripened
I no longer dally
With the dreamy enthusiasm of youth

Oh Father, the people in the village all say
I'm more and more like you
Hair getting thin like yours, balding on top
Rushing around everywhere like you
Quick to help others
Was this your hope?

和忙碌而艱苦的鄉人一樣
我們已很少談起您
父親啊，您最了解沉默
深於言語和淚水的思念
必定也能了解

Like all the best people in the village
We rarely talk about you now
Oh father! Best of all, you understood silence
Deeper than tears and words
Though these, too, you must have known well

1975

長工阿伯

長工阿伯的名字遺忘了
在為人照管的果樹園
果樹園的小木屋
長工阿伯的名字
被人遺忘好多年好多年了

在一次天災地變中
阿伯的雙親，雙雙離去
留下流著鼻涕的阿伯
給風給雨看顧

和當時臺灣的青年一樣
在一次兵禍中
阿伯的青春
埋葬在南洋構築工事
構築日本軍閥的惡夢

也在那一次兵禍中
阿伯的家小和房產
捐獻給一連串自空而降的
響亮的口號
將阿伯留給淒涼看顧

Ah-bo the Farmhand

People no longer remember his name
In the orchard he looked after for others
In the small wooden hut where he stayed
His name
Was forgotten years ago

Both his parents died
In some natural disaster
Leaving snot-nosed Ah-bo behind
In the care of wind and rain

In the ravages of war
With other young Taiwanese
Ah-bo's spring
Was buried in construction work
            in the South Pacific
Building a nightmare for Japanese warlords

And in the ravages of war
Ah-bo's wife, children, and home
Were sacrificed for an endless series
Of strident slogans
Leaving Ah-bo to be looked after by loneliness

背已佝僂，目已模糊
從南洋遣送回來之後
果樹園沉沉的暮色
如果細心，總可以聽見
忍不住的嘆息

任命運隨意作弄
任欲隱不隱的傷痕，隨意鞭撻
不知道怨恨，更不懂控訴
馴服的長工阿伯
一生都是孤兒

Back stooped, eyes bad
He was sent back from the South Pacific
If you listened hard enough
As dusk deepened in the orchard
You could always hear his endless sighs

Toyed with by fate
Indelible scars laid by the whip
Knowing no hatred nor how to accuse
Ah-bo submissively
Lived his life an orphan

1976

堤上

父親牽著我的小手，在堤上散步
堤的左方，是吾鄉的稻田
堤的右方，是濁濁滾滾的水流
吾鄉人們的歲月那樣悶悶流逝的水流
父親說：阿公也常在這種時候
放下握了一天的農具
牽著我的小手⋯⋯
我頻頻追問：阿公在哪裡呢
父親茫然望著逐漸沉淪的夕陽
不說甚麼

我牽著兒子的小手，在堤上散步
堤的左方，是吾鄉的稻田
堤的右方，是濁濁滾滾的水流
吾鄉人們的歲月那樣悶悶流逝的水流
我說：阿公也常在這種時候
放下握了一天的農具
牽著我的小手⋯⋯
兒子頻頻追問：阿公在哪裡呢
我茫然望著逐漸沉淪的夕陽
不說甚麼

Embankment

Father took my small hand in his
        as we walked along the embankment
The paddy fields of home to the left
To the right the muddy water flowed
Like time for the people of my village
Sadly the water flowed away
Father said: At times like this
Grandfather'd lay his tools aside for the day
And take me by the hand. . . .
I kept asking: Where's Grandfather now?
Father gazed at the slowly setting sun
And said nothing

I take my son's small hand in mine
        As we walk along the embankment
The paddy fields of home to the left
To the right the muddy water flows
Like time for the people of my village
Sadly, the water flows away
I say: At times like this
Grandfather'd lay his tools aside for the day
And take me by the hand. . . .
My son keeps asking: Where's Grandfather now?
I gaze at the slowly setting sun
Saying nothing

1976

過程

秧

頻頻喘著粗氣的耕牛和鐵牛
一心一意犁呀犁
翻掘每一塊泥土
三三五五分散開來的秧苗
播呀！播呀！播呀
和著大粒汗小粒汗
播下吾鄉坦蕩蕩的田地
吾鄉的人們，透早到透暝
無閒理會滿身的黑泥

陽

以那樣虔誠的跪姿
溫柔地抹去雜草
再彎下那樣虔誠的腰
灑呀！灑呀！灑呀
一桶一桶的肥料
一畚箕一畚箕的堆肥
和著日夜不眠不休的田水
和著陽光的撫慰和熬煉
灑下去！灑下去
整整齊齊排列的秧苗
也不喧呶！也不爭吵
堅忍的仰起來！仰起來

The Process

Planting Rice

Panting incessantly, ponderous oxen and tractors
Plow single-mindedly
Overturning each clod of earth
Setting out bunches of rice seedlings
Plant, plant, plant
With drops of sweat, big and small
Planting the broad, level fields of our village
The people of my village, from morning till night
Are too busy to pay attention to the mud
　　　　covering their bodies

Sun

Stooping reverently
Gently pulling weeds
Piously bending at the waist
Scatter it, scatter it all around
Bucket after bucket of fertilizer
Basket after basket of compost
Mix it in the tireless, sleepless water
　　　　in the paddy fields
Mix it with warm, soothing sunlight
Scatter it over
The rows of rice shoots
Don't argue and fight!
Grow, grow up strong!

仰

硬硬朗朗仰起來的稻禾
和著吾鄉人們全心的呵護
望呀！望呀！望呀
在焦灼的盼望中
終於伸長了身軀，伸長了脖子
伸長了一隻一隻祈禱的手臂
仰向不可測的天空求告
颱風啊！豪雨啊！蟲害啊
我們所求不多
請不要來凌虐我們

漾

一束一束金黃的稻穗
和著安分守己的一生
晃呀！晃呀！晃呀
晃著吾鄉人們
豐收的夢──
年年季季相同的夢
在吾鄉每一個曬穀場上
木訥地漾開來，漾開來
漾開吾鄉人們
壞收成望下季的期待

Look Up

Strong, sturdy plants
Are what the people of my village
        whole-heartedly await
Look, look, look!
With their anxious hopes
They stretch, craning their necks
Stretching forth one praying hand after another
Looking up at the unfathomable sky
        seeking signs of typhoon, heavy rain
                or ravenous insects
We don't ask for much
Please don't do us any harm

Bounty

Sheath after sheath of rice straw
Content with the life Heaven has bestowed
Dazzling, dazzling, dazzling!
Dazzling the people of my village
Dreams of an abundant harvest
The same dream, season after season, year after year
On all the threshing grounds in my village
The people of my village dumbly shrug it off
Dumbly shrug it off, shrug it off
A bad harvest becomes next year's hopes

1977

獸魂碑

吾鄉街路屠宰場入口處，設一獸魂碑——

碑曰：魂兮！去吧
不要轉來，不要轉來啊
快快各自去尋找
安身託命的所在
不要轉來，不要轉來啊

每逢節日，各地來的屠夫
誠惶誠恐燒香獻禮，擺上祭品
你們姑且收下吧
生而為禽畜，就要接受屠刀
不甘願甚麼呢

豬狗禽畜啊
不必哀號、不必控訴，也不必
訝異——他們一面祭拜
一面屠殺，並要求和平
他們説，這沒甚麼不對

不必哀號、不必控訴，也不必
訝異——他們一面屠殺
一面祭拜，一面恐懼你們的冤魂
回來討命；豬狗禽畜啊
魂兮！去吧

Animal Spirit Tablet

—an animal spirit tablet stands at the entrance
to the village slaughterhouse

The tablet says: "Spirits be gone!
Do not come back, do not return
Each one hurry
Find a new abode
Do not come back, do not return"

Every festival day the butchers come from all around
To fearfully burn incense and make offerings
Your mothers must accept
You are beasts born for slaughter
Why not resign yourselves?

Oh, pigs, dogs, and beasts
There's no need to cry, to accuse or
Be surprised—on the one hand they worship
On the other, they butcher
There's nothing wrong with seeking peace

There's no need to cry, to accuse, or
Be surprised, they butcher
They worship, they fear
The return of your ghosts demanding life
        pigs, dogs, and beasts
Spirits be gone!

1977

不要駭怕

阿爸和你們媽媽大聲吵嘴
只是為了讓辛酸沉重的生活
醱酵一些些甜蜜
孩子呀！不要駭怕

阿爸對世界有很多不滿
卻不敢向世界表示
只好對你們媽媽發脾氣
阿爸不是勇敢的男人

阿爸對世界有很多愛
卻不敢向世界說出來
唯恐再受到刺傷只好以這種方式
向你們媽媽傾訴
阿爸是懦弱的男人

孩子呀！不要駭怕
阿爸和你們媽媽，每一次爭吵
不過是對世界的不幸表示抗議
不過是要求世界有更多的愛

阿爸和你們媽媽，只是一對
卑微的小人物
生活這樣辛酸而沉重
只有爭吵爭吵
醱酵一些些甜蜜

Don't Be Afraid

When father and mother fight
It's only to let this hard, heavy life
Brew a little sweetness
Children, don't be afraid

Father's dissatisfied with many things
But he doesn't dare show it
It's better to lose his temper with mother
Father is not a brave man

Father loves many things in the world
But doesn't dare say a word
For fear of being hurt
It's best
To say these things to your mother
Father is a weak man

Children, don't be afraid
Each time your father and mother fight
It's a way of protesting the world's hardships
It's a way of demanding more love

Father and mother are both
Timid
With such a hard, heavy life
They can only fight
To brew a little sweetness

1977

阿爸確信

因為你們身上沾滿了泥巴
他們竟說，你們是骯髒的

因為你們不會說bye bye
他們竟說，你們是愚笨的

因為你們的粗布衣裳和赤足
他們竟說，你們是粗俗的

因為你們不喜歡誇示自己
又不善於花巧的言語
他們竟說，你們是自卑的

孩子呀！無論他們怎麼說
阿爸確信，你們是最乾淨的孩子
阿爸確信，你們深深的凝視最動人
阿爸確信，你們樸素的衣裳最漂亮

而你們要堅持
非關自卑或自傲的自尊

Father Firmly Believes

Because you're covered in dirt
They say you are dirty

Because you can't say 'bye-bye'
They say you are stupid

Because of your rough clothes and bare feet
They say you are crude

Because you don't like to brag about yourselves
And because you're not good with fancy words
They say you are ashamed of yourselves

Children, whatever they say
Father firmly believes
        you are the cleanest of children
Father firmly believes
        your deep glances are the most moving
Father firmly believes
        your simple clothes are the prettiest

You must maintain self-respect
Knowing neither shame nor pride

1977

成長

在沒有掌聲的環境中
默默成長的孩子
長大後，才不會使盡手段搶鏡頭
不習慣遭受冷落

在沒有玩具的環境中
辛勤地成長的孩子長大後，才不會將別人
也當做自己的玩具

在沒有粉飾的環境中
野樹般成長的孩子
長大後，才懂得尊重
一絲一縷的勞苦
才懂得感恩

當多數人圍著奇花異卉
齊聲讚頌
孩子呀！你們要多注視
隨處強韌地生長的小草

Growing Up

The child brought up quietly
In an environment without applause
Will, when he grows up,
Not raise himself above others
For the attention he is accustomed to

The child brought up with hard work
In an environment without toys
        will, when he grows up,
Never treat others like playthings

The child brought up like a wild tree
In an environment that's not whitewashed
Will, when he grows up,
Respect hard work and
Know how to be grateful

When people get together
To praise those strange plants and flowers
Children, take a closer look
At the tough grass growing everywhere

1977

負荷

下班之後，便是黃昏了
偶爾也望一望絢麗的晚霞
卻不再逗留
因為你們仰向阿爸的小臉
透露更多的期待

加班之後，便是深夜了
偶爾也望一望燦爛的星空
卻不再沉迷
因為你們熟睡的小臉
比星空更迷人

阿爸每日每日的上下班
有如自你們手中使勁拋出的陀螺
繞著你們轉呀轉
將阿爸激越的豪情
逐一轉為綿長而細密的柔情

就像阿公和阿媽
為阿爸織就了一生
綿長而細密的呵護
孩子呀！阿爸也沒有任何怨言
只因這是生命中
最沉重
也是最甜蜜的負荷

The Burden

It's dusk when I get off work
Sometimes I watch the beautiful twilight
But I never linger
Because your tiny upward-turning faces
Are filled with hope

Working overtime, when it's already midnight
Sometimes I look up at the clear, starry sky
But I don't indulge
Because your tiny faces, sound asleep
Are more lovely than the stars

Your father works every day
He is like the top you spin
Circling and spinning around
Turning his great affection
Into a long, loving tenderness

Just like your grandparents
Weaving a life full of love
For your father
Children, your father has no complaints
Because you are life's
Heaviest
But sweetest burden

1977

晚餐

阿媽流了一天的汗
從田裡回來
阿爸流了一天的汗
從工地回來
媽媽帶著你們，流了一天的汗
從菜園回來
並且，忙完了
瑣瑣碎碎的家務
擺上了晚餐

當雀鳥追隨著晚霞
紛紛回到庭院四周的竹枝上
吱吱喳喳報告了一天的見聞
逐漸安靜下來
當星子次第眨開
有趣的眼睛
靜聽你們紛紛爭論
今天，誰幫媽媽做最多的工作
媽媽忙完了家務
擺上了晚餐

沒有高尚的餐具做裝飾
也無須什麼擺設
我們的餐廳，在露天的庭院
寬敞而涼爽

Dinner

After sweating all day
Grandma returns from the fields
After sweating all day
Father returns from work
After sweating all day
Mother comes back with you
       from the vegetable garden
To finish all the household chores
And get dinner ready

When the birds come home at dusk
To roost in the bamboo courtyard
Chirping about the events of the day
Then slowly growing quiet
When the stars one after another
Begin to blink their curious eyes
I listen quietly as you argue
Over who helped mother most today
She is busy finishing the household chores
And getting dinner ready

We have no fancy dinnerware
Nor any need for centerpieces
Our dining room is the courtyard
       under the open sky
Spacious, cool, and comfortable

我們的晚餐，和晚風一樣
清淡而簡單
每一樣，都徐徐散發著媽媽

無微不至的愛心
孩子呀！這些香甜的蕃藷飯
這些青翠鮮嫩的蔬菜
這些菜脯和醃瓜仔
是鄉人般親切的土地
生長出來的
每一樣，都飽含著阿媽
費心照顧的汗水
星光與月光，相互輝映下
看你們吃得那樣起勁
阿媽和媽媽的笑容，多燦爛

Our dinner is like the evening breeze
Simple and plain
Always alike, each dish shows

Mother's thoughtful, loving heart
Children, the tasty potatoes and rice
These tender greens
These vegetables and pickled cucumbers
All come from the soil
We live so close to
Always alike, each dish contains
Grandma's hard work
Under the light of the stars and moon
Watching you eat with such joy
Grandma's smile and mother's
   Are both so bright

1978

阿爸偶爾寫的詩

和我們生長的鄉村一樣
不習慣裝腔作勢
阿爸偶爾寫的詩
沒有英雄式的宣言
也沒有輝煌的歌頌
只是一些些
粗俗而笨重的腳印

和我們日日親近的泥土一樣
不喜歡說漂亮話
阿爸偶爾寫的詩
沒有繽紛耀眼的光采
也沒有華麗迷人的詞句
只是一些些
安分而無甜味的汗水

孩子呀！阿爸偶爾寫的詩
無意引來任何讚嘆
也不必憑藉任何掌聲
和我們每天在一起勞動的村民一樣
對深奧的大道理，非常陌生
又欠缺曲曲折折的奇思妙想
只是一些些
對生命忍抑不住的感激與掛慮

The Poems Father Occasionally Writes

The poems father occasionally writes
Are like the village we grew up in
Where no one puts on airs
The poems father occasionally writes
Make no heroic declarations
Are not brilliant song
Just a few
Rough, awkward footprints

The poems father occasionally writes
Are like the soil we live close to
Despising all sweet talk
Never flashy or eye-catching
Never charming
Just the salty
Sweat of contentment

Children, the poems father occasionally writes
Never seek to win praise
Or applause
Like the people of our village
     we work with every day
They are strangers to profound truths
They lack marvelous thoughts
Just some hearty
Praise and a few anxieties about life

1978

寒夜

抱著你，拍啊拍
輕輕的拍
你卻將阿爸書桌上的鋼筆和詩稿
一件一件拿起來玩耍
一件一件拋到地上

背著你，搖啊搖
輕輕的搖
你卻在阿爸背上，呀呀抗議
使勁扯著阿爸的頭髮

孩子呀！安靜的睡吧
在這樣寒冷的深夜
一切如此寂靜
你為什麼還不安睡

難道你也知道
孤燈下，阿爸孤單的苦思和低吟
是最最徒然的愚行嗎
你也知道阿爸平淡的詩句
是多少苦難的焦慮
熬鍊出來的嗎

Cold Night

Holding you
Patting you softly
You pick up father's pen and poems
From the desk, playing with them
You drop them on the floor

Carrying you on my back
Gently swaying
On father's back you protest
Pulling his hair

Children, sleep tight
On this cold, dark night
With everything so quiet
Why can't you sleep?

Perhaps you, too, know
Father's useless, foolish behavior
Sitting up alone beneath a lamp
       Racking his brains, softly reciting
Do you know how much suffering
Goes into making
Each simple line?

夜已這樣深，這樣寒冷
關掉燈，我們去睡吧
孩子呀！長大後
千萬不要像阿爸
讓絲絲寒氣，時時折磨自己

Ah, it's already late, so cold
Turn off the light and go to bed
Children, when you grow up
Don't ever be like your father
Wearing himself away in the cold

1978

你也走了

終於，你也走了
你寄來的賀年片上
每一處異國的風景
正如傳說中那樣美麗而陌生
望著我低低喟嘆
終於，你也走了

去年秋季，你來我住的鄉間小遊
曾經透露出
伯父已費盡心思
在異國購置了不少房產
在異國的銀行，存了不少錢款
而你即將去定居

我曾疑惑的問你
你出去做甚麼呢
為了學業嗎？為了考察嗎
我料想不到，你竟說
有辦法的人，不是紛紛走了
或是牽親引戚
拿綠卡，隨時準備走嗎

你是否也是
有辦法的人
我只記得，昔日的校園裡
你曾以多麼沉悒的激情

You Too Have Left

In the end, you too have left
On the New Year's cards you send home
Scenic spots in foreign lands
As beautiful and strange as the legends
Looking, I sigh
In the end, you left too

Last autumn you came back to visit
You let me know
Your father racked his brains
      making plans
Buying a house and property overseas
Depositing money in foreign banks
And that's where you plan to stay

I recall once asking
What you do there
Study, research
I didn't know, you finally said
Aren't people always trying to find ways
      to leave here
Dragging in relatives
For green cards, preparing to leave?

I don't know if you are one of those
Who always finds a way
I only remember how back in school
You pledged with me
To regain the dignity of this small piece of land

和我一再約定
要為被殖民過的
受盡欺凌和屈辱的蕃藷土地
爭回尊嚴；你的激情
時時鼓舞著容易頹喪的我
時時溫暖著在鄉村耕作的我

而今，你終於也走了
攜著你的妻小
帶著異國的永久居留權
悄悄的離開了
離開辛苦地生你、養你、育你
急切需要已經長大的你
為伊打拚的這塊土地

終於，你也走了
你還會回來嗎
在異族歧視的眼神中
你切得斷和我們這塊土地的血緣嗎
我們整個民族的苦難和傷痛
你能輕易忘記嗎
你有甚麼理由，放逐自己呢

This rough land which had been colonized,
Bullied, and humiliated
I only remember your enthusiasm
Encouraging me, who is so easily depressed
Bringing warmth to me, a farmer

But now, in the end you too have left
With your wife and children
Holding a foreign residence permit
You quietly left
The bitter land that bore you,
            raised you, taught you
Provided you everything you needed
Now needs you to fight for her

In the end you too have left
Will you be back?
Under the eyes of another people
Will you cut the ties that bind?
And your descendants?
Can you so easily forget
Their suffering and pain?
Why must you exile yourself?
I can't believe it
To live in exile
Are you willing to forsake
The nationality your ancestors have held
            for thousands of years?

是的，你終於也走了
從美麗而陌生的風景上
移開迷惑而悲傷的眼光
望出去
無數的農民，仍在農田辛勤地流汗
無數的工人，仍在工廠勞苦地操作
無數無數各階層的人們
仍在忙碌而堅定的工作
和我一樣，懇切的盼著你
盼著有辦法的手足
為生長我們的土地
認真打拚

Yes, you too have left
I look up from the strange and lovely scene
          on the card
And look outside
I am confused and saddened
The many farmers I see still sweat in the fields
The many workers I see still labor in the factories
Countless classes of people
Still busily working
Like myself, we all hope
That our brothers like you can find a way
To work hard
For this land that bore us

1978

美國籍

在我們這個偏僻的鄉間
你是少有的
「來來來，來臺大
去去去，去美國」的優秀人才
讓鄰里欽羨地傳誦
讓故鄉殷切地盼望

然而，聽說你也入了美國籍
生活非常忙碌
為了分期付款購買的房子
和一本信用卡
很少有時間寫家書
你一定有不得已的苦衷吧

在家鄉，年老的母親
也一直很忙碌
為了我們的學費
為了一季一季永遠做不完的農事
為了你出國時
留給家裡的一大筆債務

你出去的那年年底
和風雨坎坷、烈日霜寒
拚鬥一生的父親，車禍去世
將整個困厄的生活
交給母親承擔

American Citizenship

Out here in the sticks
You rarely encounter such genius:
"Come, come, come to Taiwan U
Go, go, go to the US"
Words passed with envy from mouth to mouth
Giving the hometown high hopes

Then I heard you've become an American citizen
You're very busy
With house payments
Credit cards
You rarely have time to write home
You must know unspeakable hardship
At home, mother
Is busy as always
Covering our tuition
Doing never-ending farm work
          season after season
For you to study abroad and
Leave the family in debt

You ought to remember
          at the end of the year you left
Father, who struggled all his life
In wind and rain, in scorching sun and bitter cold
Died in a car accident
Leaving all life's difficulties
To mother, who can't even read

十餘年了，不識字的母親
一到晚上，都有一大堆話
不外乎是永無止盡的牽掛
要我寫信告訴你

而我更想告訴你
每逢親戚鄰居辦喜事
母親也都一再吩咐
要我在禮券上
寫上你的名字
只因為，你是母親的大兒子
我們的大哥

雖然，你離開落後的家鄉
竟已十餘年
而且也入了美國籍
雖然，你每封寄回來的航空郵簡
對我們幾個弟妹的不成器
既嘆息，又生氣

是的，我們都很令你失望
正如艱苦地養育我們長大的
這塊蕃藷土地
不能帶給你光采和榮耀
因為我們不願親近
驕傲的ABC
只願在自己的家鄉
默默地工作，勤奮地流汗

For more than ten years,
        From morning till night
Our illiterate mother
Has had so much
She wanted me to write and tell you
—how she worried about you

And I ought to tell you
Every time there's a wedding in the village
Mother insists
I write your name
In the register
Because you are the eldest son
Our older brother

You left your backward hometown
More than ten years ago
To become an American citizen
In every airmail letter home
You express your disappointment and anger
At your unsuccessful brothers and sisters

Yes, we've all disappointed you
You're ashamed of us
Like this small plot of land
This stupid plot of land
Which provides you no sense of pride or glory
Because we are unwilling to study
Those proud ABCs
We're only willing to work, struggle and sweat in silence
In our homeland
I heard you've become an American citizen

聽說，你也入了美國籍
生活非常忙碌
你一定有不得已的苦衷吧
你可曾像母親這樣惦念你
惦念著逐漸衰老的母親
我們從小吃慣的
又好吃又便宜的蕃藷
可曾在你的記憶中出現
你在遙遠的異國
為誰而忙碌，為甚麼而忙碌

You're very busy
You must have suffered great hardship
I don't know if you miss mother
            The way she misses you
She's growing older thinking about you
Do you ever think about
The potatoes we ate as kids?
They were cheap and tasty
I don't know why
You are so busy in that foreign land
And for whom

1978

早餐桌旁

早餐桌旁
從未感覺到如此孤單
草草嚥下速食麵
便坐著發愣
怔怔地回味家裡的餐桌上
散發的香味

你來信說
我們家庭院前的菜園
蔬菜瓜果，皆已成熟
想你每天早晨
在初昇的朝陽照耀下
彎下腰輕輕採摘
我隱隱聞到滿園清新的氣息

那是我離家前
一鋤一鋤掘鬆泥土
細心的種植
或許長得並不肥美
卻是吸收了不少我的汗水
你一定會珍惜

早餐桌旁
從未感到如此孤單
草草嚥下速食麵
便坐著發愣
孩子們圍坐餐桌旁
吵吵嚷嚷的聲音
在我耳際不斷縈繞

At the Breakfast Table

At the breakfast table
I never felt so lonely
Hurriedly I slurp down instant noodles
Then sit staring into space
Thinking about our dinner table at home
And the wonderful aromas

Your letter said that
The vegetables in the garden
In front of the house are ready
I think of you each morning
Stooping to pick them
Under the newly risen sun
I can almost smell the freshness

I loosened the soil with a shovel
And carefully planted the seeds
Before I left
They may not be the finest
But they've had a share of my sweat
I'm sure you will prize them

At the breakfast table
I never felt so lonely
Hurriedly I slurp down instant noodles
Then sit staring vacantly into space
The chatter of the children
Around the dinner table
Lingers in my ears

1981

我不和你談論

我不和你談論詩藝
不和你談論那些糾纏不清的隱喻
請離開書房
我帶你去廣袤的田野走走
去看看遍處的幼苗
如何沉默地奮力生長

我不和你談論人生
不和你談論那些深奧玄妙的思潮
請離開書房
我帶你去廣袤的田野走走
去撫觸清涼的河水
如何沉默地灌溉田地

我不和你談論社會
不和你談論那些痛徹心肺的爭奪
請離開書房
我帶你去廣袤的田野走走
去探望一群一群的農民
如何沉默地揮汗耕作

你久居鬧熱滾滾的都城
詩藝呀！人生呀！社會呀
已爭辯了很多
這是急於播種的春日
而你難得來鄉間
我帶你去廣袤的田野走走
去領略領略春風
如何溫柔地吹拂著大地

I Won't Discuss It with You

I won't discuss the art of poetry with you
I won't discuss involved metaphors with you
Let's leave the study
Let me take you for a walk in the broad fields
Covered with young shoots to see
How they silently strive to grow

I won't discuss life with you
I won't discuss profound and mysterious thoughts with you
Let's leave the study
Let me take you for a walk in the broad fields
To touch the cool, clear river water
And see how it silently irrigates the paddy fields

I won't discuss society with you
I won't discuss how painfully people vie with each other
Let's leave the study
Let me take you for a walk in the broad fields
To visit groups of farmers
To see how they silently wipe away their sweat

Long have you lived in the hub-hub of the city
Poetry! Life! Society!
Have all been debated
It is spring, a time eager for planting
And you rarely come to the village
Let me take you for a walk in the broad fields
To feel the spring breeze
And how it blows warm and gentle over the land

1982

大度山

我是必定要回去的

在愛荷華
楓紅遍處、遊子遍處
深秋的異國小鎮
在我暫時租住的公寓
把酒傾談家鄉事
一番唏噓、一番激憤之後
你常堅決的表示

我是必定要回去的

在大度山
清幽的林木下，無數學子
神采煥發的來來往往
深秋的校區
在你將永久居住的宿舍
緊緊握住你溫熱的手掌
你真的回來了

你不羨慕異國的安逸嗎
你不嚮往過客
來去自如的光采嗎
紛紛驚慌走避的暗潮
正在家鄉盛行
是甚麼催促你逆流而回

你平靜的回答我：出去
本就是為了回來

Dadu Mountain

I'll certainly be returning

In Iowa
Red leaves everywhere, travelers everywhere
Overseas in a small town in late autumn
In the apartment I'm renting
Drinking and talking about home every night
After a bout of sobbing and anger
You firmly state

I'll certainly be returning

On Dadu Mountain
In the quiet and secluded forest countless students
Come and go in high spirits
The campus in late autumn
In the dorm where you will reside
I tightly grasp your hand
And moved, I say: you've really come back

Don't you envy the ease and comfort overseas?
Don't you long to be a passing visitor
Smoothly coming and going with splendor?
An undercurrent of panicked flight
Runs high in the homeland
What prompts you to come home against the tide?

Calmly you answer: To leave
Is to return

回來向深受創痛的家鄉
證明：並非所有的遊子
都是為了逃避家鄉的災難
去與回之間，只不過多了
對家鄉更痛切的憂慮
對家鄉更深刻的眷戀

與其在異邦
徒然放言悲憤的論調
不如回來
燃放一些光亮，一些溫暖
暗潮洶湧的滔滔濁流中
我們不可能是砥柱
只是要深受創痛的家鄉
相信：多少的年輕遊子
情願捨棄安逸
回來，擁抱家鄉的悲苦和榮耀

在大度山
緊緊握住你厚實的手掌
猶如緊緊握住
溫和而堅定的信誓

Returning to a deeply suffering homeland
To prove that not all who live abroad
Are fleeing home's disasters
Between leaving and returning is nothing more than
A more intense pain for home
A deeper attachment to home

While living in a foreign land
Rather than express your argument and
Bear the terrible longing for home in vain
One might as well come back to kindle light and warmth
In the turbid flow of the undercurrent
There's no way for us to hold out
Only we must bear up for the deeply suffering homeland
To believe that the many young who live abroad
Willingly give up ease and comfort
To return and embrace the sadness and glory of home

On Dadu Mountain
I grasp your broad hand
As if tightly grasping a
Warm and steadfast oath

1983

你不必再操煩

母親，你終於可以和你的田地
閒閒過日；不必再操煩稻作
有無缺水、有無欠肥、有無疾病蟲害
不必再趕時趕陣犁田、插秧、除草……

你不必再操煩
稻穗有無結實飽滿、有無颱風來襲
收割期會不會遇上滂沱雨水
或是穀價如何起起落落

母親，你從年少依托田地
整整一甲子而有餘
度過戰亂、度過匱乏，也經歷了
工商文明快速變遷的再三衝擊

一方稻田裡，日日重疊的厚實足印
一季接一季，從不缺席
你確實已年老
但仍有足夠力氣自給自足

母親，你實在難以理解
你一粒一粒都這樣惜寶的米糧
只要仰賴國際強權的傾銷
並要求自己的田地休耕，任其荒廢

You Don't Need to Worry Anymore

Mother, finally you and your fields can
Rest, you don't need to worry
If there's enough water or fertilizer,
        or about disease and insects
Plowing, planting, or weeding to a seasonal rhythm

There's no need to worry
About the ripening grain
        about typhoons hitting
About pouring rain at harvest time
Or the ups and downs in grain prices

Mother, ever since you were young, you've relied on the fields
For more than sixty years
They have seen
War, poverty, and recurring assaults
By a rapidly changing industrial civilization

Fields trudged across day after day by sturdy feet
Season after season, never absent
You are old now
But you can still take care of yourself

Mother, it's difficult for you to understand
You value each grain of rice
But must look to the foreign powers to dump goods
And demands that your land lie fallow, neglected

你實在無從想像
田地的價值，並非為了耕作
而是用來炒作
辛勤一世人的老農，竟然是
台灣經濟發展的拖累

猶如承受過肥料換穀、田賦繳穀
半夜捉人催繳水租種種驚嚇壓榨
母親，你唯有自我調適
領取些微恩惠補助
和你的田地閒閒過日吧

你不必再操煩稻作，也無從擔憂
總有一天，進口糧食斷絕
而台灣島嶼已找不到農民
甚至，找不到可供耕作的田地

You really can't imagine
The value of land, not for planting
But for speculating
A generation of hard-working old farmers is
A burden to Taiwan's economic development

Mother, you just have to get used to
Receiving supplementary income from the government
And leisurely passing your days in your fields
The way you had to accept fertilizer, new grain, land taxes,
            handing over again
Paying for water use in the middle of the night
            to the tyrannical fee collector

You don't have to work or worry
There'll come a day when grain imports stop
But there won't be a farmer found
            then on the entire island
Nor a tillable field

1994

黑色土壤

從幼童跟隨母親去農田
撿稻穗、拾蕃藷、採野菜
從年少跟隨母親去農田
割田草、挑秧苗、巡田水
從成年跟隨母親去農田
駛犁、插秧、施肥

在濁水溪畔廣大溪埔地
每一步踩踏田土的足跡
每一個貼近田土的身影
每一滴滴落田土的汗水
紛紛萌生根鬚、茂盛枝葉
凝結信靠大地的愛戀

一季一季平靜耕作
濁水溪畔每一寸黑色土壤
由芽而苗而綠意盎然
陪伴母親一生的寄託
豐富了我的年少和壯年

那是什麼花、什麼作物
又是如何日日夜夜緩慢成長
速食文化衝擊下
土生土長的家鄉子弟
竟茫茫然面對我的詢問
我是多麼驚愕

Black Soil

As a child I followed mother in the fields
Gleaning grain, gathering potatoes, picking wild vegetables
As a youth I followed mother in the fields
Cutting grass, carrying rice sprouts, checking the water level
As an adult I followed mother in the fields
Plowing, planting rice sprouts, spreading fertilizer

On the broad plain beside the Zhuoshui River
Every muddy footprint from the rice fields
Every human shadow along the rice fields
Every drop of sweat fallen on the rice fields
Sprouts roots, stems and leaves
Coalescing the love of the trusted earth

Season after season
Every inch of black soil beside the Zhuoshui River
From sprout to seeding to abundant green
Entrusted to a lifetime of mother's care
Enriching my youth and the prime of my life

What flower is that, what kind of crop
Grows slowly day and night?
Plagued by fast-food culture
The local kids
Respond with blank looks
Leaving me dumbfounded

還有誰記取
從牛犁牛耙到耕耘機
從秧盆秧桿到插秧機
從鐮刀打穀箱到割稻機
步步艱辛的稻作演變
將無地可耕而棄置

我的足跡、我的身影和汗水
牢牢連結廣大溪埔地
無論擴張又擴張的經濟風潮
如何刺痛我信靠大地的愛戀
我仍願緊密守護
每一寸黑色土壤

And who remembers going
From ox to power tiller
From basin and dibble to transplanting machine
From scythe and winnower to mechanical harvester
The slow and difficult work of farming will be forsaken
Having no land left to farm

But my footprints, shadow, and sweat
Are firmly linked with the broad plain beside the Zhuoshui River
Regardless of how wave after wave of economic expansion
Has harmed my love for the trusted earth
I continue to closely guard
Every inch of black soil

1996

土地公

滿滿一大卡車砂石
轟隆隆傾倒而下
又一大片青青農地，迅即消失
田頭小小土地廟，也深深掩埋

驚惶逃離的土地公
繞著隆起的砂石堆黯然徘徊
恍恍惚惚望見
每一粒砂石，似乎都很熟識

那不是世代先民
長年累月在這片溪埔地
——彎腰撿拾而起的嗎
透入砂石的掌紋和血汗
仍分明可辨

開墾，歷經漫長年月
開發，不過短短時日
滿滿一大卡車砂石轟隆隆傾倒而下
大舉吞噬農鄉
生生不息的作物命脈
便永遠沉埋歷史底層

Earth God

A truck
Dumps another load of gravel
Another large patch of green farmland disappears
The small shrine to the Earth God at the field's edge
        lies buried

The Earth God, who fled in fright
Circles the pile of gravel,
        paces up and down, downcast
Stares in confusion at each seemingly
Familiar stone

Wasn't it our ancestors
Who over the years on the banks of this river
Bent over to pick up these stones?
The lines of their hands, their sweat and blood
Can still be seen

It took forever to open up this wasteland for farming
Development occurred overnight
A truck thunderously dumps loads of gravel
Swallowing up huge tracts of farmland
The lifeblood of an endless succession of crops
Sinks to the bottom of the past

無田守護的土地公
再無香火繚繞
終於被迫流離失所
隱隱聽見政客與財團
聯手歡呼
歡呼完成了「農地釋放」

也許萬頃良田將完全淪陷
再也無從尋覓
縱橫交錯的田畦和溝渠
吾鄉的子弟
終將懷著漂泊的靈魂
無依地流浪

With no fields to protect
And no offerings of incense
The Earth God will be forced to wander, homeless
Faintly hearing the politicians and tycoons
Join hands and cheer
The completion of the "release of agricultural land"

Perhaps all the farmland
Will fall into enemy hands
The criss-crossed fields and ditches
Will be lost forever
The children of my village
Will become homesick spirits, drifting
Wandering helplessly

1996

賣田

終於蓋下最後一個印鑑
交出土地權狀
鮮紅的印痕，有如心頭泌出的血漬
化作老淚潸潸
滑過黧黑的臉龐

這幾分田產
你承續了父祖滿懷虔誠
彎腰耕植、流汗撒種
一輩子守住生生不息的作物

你不曾留意工商文明
洶湧的浪潮
如何衝擊四周田地
如何掀起詭譎的媚惑
迅快捲走子孫的足跡

過了今夜，土地即將轉手
星空下，燃燒稻梗的餘燼
還在田裡明滅閃爍
你恍恍惚惚坐在田頭
聽圳溝水流嗚嗚咽咽
細數一一流逝的夢想

細數這一片寬厚土壤
孕育每一粒種子
萌芽、抽長、餵飽穀實

Selling the Fields

Finally, the last seal is affixed
Turning over ownership of the land
A red scar, red as blood from the heart
Old tears trickle down
A dark face

With these patches of fields
You continued your father's and his father's piety
Stooping to plant, sweating and sowing seeds
A life spent keeping crops growing

You never paid attention to industrialized society
How the surging waves
Broke around your fields
How its beguiling trickery
Swept away your descendants footprints

After tonight, the land will change hands
Under the starry sky, the embers of burning rice stubble
Still glow in the fields
Absent-mindedly, you sit by the fields
Listening to the sobbing murmurs of water in the ditch
Counting past dreams

Counting each grain of rice
Borne by this generous land
Sprouting, growing, nourishing grain

當微風輕拂稻浪婆娑款擺
是你多麼傾心的寄託

然而這些夢想和寄託
就在轉賣手續中
化作沙沙作響的嘲笑

據說只需幾次文書往返
只需幾番地目變更的把戲
填上砂石、混入泥漿、疊架高樓
這一小筆田地
即將隆起繁華夢幻

而你終究必須起身離去
就像田裡燃燒的稻梗
完全熄滅了火苗
你永遠無力挽留
種子的最後一聲吶喊

The waves of grain stirred by the breeze
Is where you placed your hopes

Then these dreams and hopes
In the process of making the sale
Become a mocking laugh

People say it only takes a few documents
A few tricks for the transfer
Cover the land with gravel, pour concrete, put up a high-rise
And illusions of prosperity
Rise on this small plot of land

But finally you must rise and depart
Like the burning stubble in the fields
When it goes out
You'll always be powerless to press
The last cry of the seeds to stay

1996

寫詩的最大悲哀

寫詩的最大悲哀
不在於困苦思索
不在於寤寐追求
不在於字斟句酌的琢磨

寫詩的最大悲哀
不在於長年寂寞完成了詩作
無任何回響
不在於些少聲名
引來同輩冷冷的嘲諷

寫詩的最大悲哀
不在於心靈深處
不時洶湧衝撞的詩情
無力一一制伏

寫詩的最大悲哀
不在於直接逼視人生的缺憾
又無補於現實
不在於必須隱忍人世的傷痛
壓縮再壓縮

即使心頭淌血，也要耐心尋找
沉澱下來的血漬

那麼，寫詩的最大悲哀
也許是除了寫詩
不知道還有什麼方式
可以對抗生命的龐大悲哀

The Saddest Thing about Writing Poetry

The saddest thing about writing poetry
Is not racking one's brain
Is not its pursuit, sleepless in bed
Is not in the polish of weighing every word

The saddest thing about writing poetry
Is not the hours of loneliness spent completing a poem
Which meets with no response
Is not the small successes
That meet with jeers from one's peers

The saddest thing about writing poetry
Is not the depth of the soul
Constantly surging with poetic sentiment
That cannot be controlled

The saddest thing about writing poetry
Is not intently watching the flaws of the human world
That cannot be remedied in reality
Is not having to forbear the pains of the human world
As they bear down again and again

Even if the heart drips blood, patiently searching
For blood's sediment is a must

Well, the saddest thing about writing poetry
Is perhaps not knowing any other way
To combat the great sadness of life
Other than by writing poetry

1997

油菜花田

初冬的陽光，暖暖撫照
盛放的油菜花田
慵懶地躺臥
躺成黃絨絨的寬敞花毯
補償田野長年的勞累

一隻一隻蛾蝶，翩翩穿梭
這一大片燦爛金黃
和童年嬉戲的夢境
交織飛舞

我禁不住停緩腳步
依傍著青澀香氣輕輕躺下
靜靜尋索、無須寄望收成的閒適
有否妥切詩句來描繪

我禁不住低聲詢問
雜沓的車聲，可否遠離
急速氾濫的聲光資訊，可否遠離
遠離消費文明的追趕

就這樣跟隨天邊雲霞的寧謐
跟隨滿天月光與星光
放任恬淡自足的夢想
一起去遨遊

Fields of Rapeseed Flowers

Early winter light's warm caress
Fields of rapeseed flowers in bloom
Lay listlessly
Form a broad velvety yellow flowering carpet
Compensation for laboring year-long in the fields

Butterflies and moths flutter back and forth
This stretch of golden yellow flowers
Are woven into a dance
With the dream world of childhood play

I can't help but slow my pace
Gently lie down amidst the green, astringent fragrance
Quietly seeking   the quiet and comfort
        Free from harvest's expectations
To see if a line of poetry may come

I can't help but ask in a whisper
Can't the unruly sound of traffic be left far behind
Can't the rapid flood of sound and visual information be left far
behind
Leave far behind the pursuit of consumer culture

Follow the tranquility of beautiful clouds on the horizon
Follow the moonlight and starlight filling the sky
Leave the dream of contentment
And journey away together

待春風春雨重臨田野
耕耘機勢必無暇留意
閒散開放的油菜花
卻是我永遠的憧憬

Waiting for the wind and rain of spring to visit the fields again
The power tiller no doubt will be too busy to notice
The leisurely blossoming rapeseed flowers
Are in fact, what I always long for

1997

沿海一公里

——憂傷西海岸之三

又一紙開發公文
號令電鋸全面殺伐
數萬株挺直的木麻黃，相繼仆倒

無處落腳的海鳥
牠們不會說話，只能嘎嘎啼叫
在昏暗暮色中來回盤旋

又一段海岸線
頓時失去屏障
灰撲撲的風砂趁勢席捲
破落的小漁村

我的哀傷飄蕩在海線城鎮
每一聲喟嘆，都化作渴切願望
如果沿海一公里
耐風耐旱的防風林無盡綿延

開展茂盛根鬚抓住砂土
搖曳青青枝葉
像飄在風中的綠圍巾
阻隔來自海洋的風寒

One Kilometer of Coastline

—concerns for the West Coast 3

Another development memo
Orders the saws to clear
Thousands of trees, felling them one after another

The seabirds have no place to perch
They cannot speak, so all they do is clamor
Circling in the darkening light of dusk

Another stretch of coastline
Instantly loses a screen
With an opening, the wind-whipped sand
Engulfs a run-down fishing village

Every sigh from my coastal
Cities and villages set sadly adrift
Becomes a thirsty longing
For a kilometer-long stretch of coastline
      Windbreaks to withstand the wind and dryness

They spread dense roots to hold the sand in place
Wave green branches
Like green scarves blowing in the wind
Blocking the cold wind from the sea

啊，如果沿海一公里
鬱鬱蔥蔥的防風林
和翠綠山嶺相互呼應
將美麗島嶼，暖暖環抱

O, if only a kilometer-long stretch of shoreline
Windbreaks, green and luxuriant
Can work in concert with the green mountains
To protect the environment of this lovely isle

1999

他還年輕

他還年輕
雖然在深邃的海洋底下
岩石的湧動已經好幾億年了
高溫、擠壓、崩裂、沉積
每一次變動，都是艱苦的淬煉
讓沙泥變質成為最堅貞的母岩

他還在成長
從藍色的波浪間緩緩上升
站成東北亞洲最英挺的高峰
冰雪像利刃，切割過起伏的稜線
白玉一般潔淨的紋理
是島嶼上最溫柔的面容

種子不斷迸裂
生命的精氣，在雲霧繚繞處瀰漫
蒼蒼莽林正在苗壯
像上天的庇蔭
那慈愛恩澤，從天頂綿延直到平原草坡

水流從來沒有停歇、冰晶狀
從石英片岩的縫隙滲出
細小的溪澗，匯聚成雄渾的大河
土地的乳汁汩汩
孕育果實甜蜜、穀粒飽滿

He's Still Young

He's still young
Although rock has been extruded for millions of years
Deep down at the bottom of the sea
High temperatures, pressure, fissures, and sediment
Each change, a difficult tempering
Making the metamorphosis of sand and clay
            into the most constant of mother rock

He's still growing
Rising slowly amid the blue waves
Standing to become the most prominent peak in northeast Asia
Ice and snow like a sharp knife have carved the undulating
                mountain ridge
Veins like pure-white jade
The island's most tender countenance

Seeds never cease splitting
The vitality of life spreads in places where cloud-mist winds
Vast and hazy jungles thrive
Like a heavenly shelter
Pervading benevolence stretching zenith to grassy plains

The water never stops flowing, ice crystals form
Seep from quartz and schist fissures
Small mountain streams converge to form great seas
The milk of the land gurgles
Nurturing the sweetness of fruit, the fullness of grain

高山族人，在雪融之後的溪澗旁
勞動、生活、繁衍
生命的步履像躍動的歌舞
旋律是泠泠的流水
姿態是翻飛的樹葉
森林的好鄰居，可以相依相伴千萬年

我們的玉山，他正年輕
雖然一再承受激烈的震盪
烈火焚燒、還有斧頭利鋸烙下的傷痕
和共同走過艱苦的台灣一樣，深刻的痛
讓他成長、再成長

Mountain tribespeople, beside the streams after the snow melts
Labor, live, and proliferate
The steps of life resemble a leaping dance and song
The melody is cold flowing water
Postured with fluttering leaves
Good forest neighbors rely on each other for thousands of years

Our Jade Mountain, he is still young
Although constantly rocked by quakes
Scorched with fire, and scarred with axes
Like Taiwan which has experienced hardships and deep suffering
Let him grow and grow

2001

春寒特別沁冷

—寄瘂弦

那年你從河南老家探親回台北
攜帶了一包瓜菓種籽
要我在自家園圃培育
我小心翼翼澆水看顧
嫩綠的莖枝細葉日日伸展
滿心盼望每一株芽苗
接受這片土壤豐厚的滋養

不知是你帶來的品種
不適應我家鄉的氣候水土
還是照料方式出了差錯
剛開出細小的黃色花朵
尚未結菓落籽
竟一一枯萎

正要向你說明
聽聞你已辦妥移民手續
舉家拔營遷居加拿大
我的抱憾增添無比惆悵

你曾數度踏臨
我立足耕作的鄉間
長年支持我從土地萌發的詩作
我也常去你都會的寓所
徹夜聽你訴說
鄉愁的唏噓、詩藝的豐采
從不掩飾近乎孺慕的敬仰

A Chill Permeates the Spring

—for Ya Hsien

The year you returned to Taipei
    from visiting family in your old home of Henan
You brought back a bag of melon seeds
For me to grow in my garden
I watered them carefully and looked after them
The tender green stems and fine leaves spread by the day
Every shoot filled with hope
Generously nourished by the soil of this land

I don't know if the variety you brought back was
Unfit for the weather, water and soil of my homeland
Or if something about my care was wrong
As they started putting forth small yellow flowers
They dropped without forming fruit
Each one withered

But when I wanted to explain things
I heard you had finished immigrating
Pulled up stakes for Canada
Making my regrets all the sadder

So many times you visited
The home where I have a footing and a farm
Over the years, supporting the poems sprung from my land
Often did I visit you in the big city
Listening to you deep into the night as you spoke of
The sadness of homesickness, the rich pickings of ars poetica
Never glossing over my loving admiration and reverence for you.

你只是悄悄離去
沒有漂流或放逐的張揚
但你終究如河南老家的瓜菓
不能在島上深深扎根嗎

春寒特別沁冷的日子
我在自家庭院
親手種植的小樹園，撿拾枯枝
燃起一堆小小火光，取暖
揣想你在異國寬闊的森林
閒適漫遊的步履
恍惚中忽然聽見
橋橋大嫂切除了大半的肺葉
緊促的咳嗽聲
從你的短箋持續傳來
聲聲衝擊著我
逐漸抵擋不住寒氣的初老身軀

我在自家小樹園
你在異國寬闊的森林
相繼老去的歲月中
相隔如此迢遙
請你和橋橋多珍重
待天氣回暖
期望再來鄉間走走

You left quietly
With no announcement of wandering or banishment
But in the end were you like the melon seeds
          from your old home in Henan
Unable to put down roots on this island?

On days when a chill permeates spring
In the courtyard of my home
I make a small fire for warmth
From the twigs I gather in the small grove of trees I'd planted,
Imagine you in the vast forest in a foreign land
Amid the footsteps during a quiet and comfortable stroll
Suddenly the pressing coughs of sister-in-law Qiao Qiao,
          who had half a lung removed
Kept coming from your short letter
Each sound striking me
Gradually I can't keep the chill from my ageing body

I'm in my small grove of trees
You in the broad forest of a foreign land
As in days gone by
Separated by such a great distance
Please, you and Qiao Qiao take care of each other
Wait till it warms up
In hopes that you can come and walk here again

2004

落葉

傍晚在自家小樹園
日常休憩，靜看葉片謝幕前
最後的舞姿
又如流連依依的揮別

偶有一截枯枝
啵一聲掉落
躺臥在鋪滿落葉的地面
我彷彿聽見
辭行的喟嘆，非常輕

拿起竹耙，掃成堆
像例行性清掃逝去的日子
抬起頭，落葉迴旋又紛紛
才正要輕吁出聲
赫然發現，每一截枯枝
是新芽萌發的預告
每一片落葉，輕輕鬆手
都是為了讓位給新生

如同逐年老去的我
在每一張童稚的面容
煥發的青春裡
找到生命延續的歡欣

Falling Leaves

While taking my usual rest
In the tree grove at dusk, I quietly watch
The last dancing leaves before they fall
And how they reluctantly wave goodbye

Occasionally a withered branch will
Snap and fall
To lie on the ground carpeted by leaves
I can almost hear
The sigh of goodbye, ever so gentle

I take up my bamboo rake, rake them into a pile
As if sweeping away the departed days of routine affairs
Looking up, I see the falling leaves spin and flutter
And on the point of sighing
I am amazed to discover each withered branch
Is a herald announced by new shoots
Every falling leaf gently loosens its grip
To make way for new life

I am no different as I age
In every young face
Burning with youth
I find the joy of life's continuity

2005

森林墓園

種一棵樹，取代一座墳墓
植一片樹林，代替墳場
樹身周邊闢一小方花圃
亡者的骨灰依傍樹頭
埋葬或撒入花叢
送別的親友圍繞
合掌追思、默念、話別

不一定清明節日
想念的時陣
相招前來澆澆水
貼近樹身輕撫擁抱
也許可以聽見
亡者仍在身旁，諄諄叮嚀

別忘了欣賞好風景
當微風沙沙拂動枝葉
樹梢上，群鳥飛躍鳴唱
仿若相互打招呼

陽光星月殷勤相伴
樹與樹，聲息相通
像是亡者的記憶
相牽在地底
新枝嫩芽盡情綻放
各自印證修行成果

Tree Cemetery

Plant a tree in place of a grave
Plant a patch of trees in place of a cemetery
Put a flowerbed around each tree
Lay the ashes of the deceased to rest by the stump
Buried or scattered among the flowers
Surrounded by mourning friends and family
Hands clasped in remembrance, contemplation, and farewell

Remembrance need not be the time
Relegated to the Tomb-sweeping Festival
Come together and water the tree
Press close to it, caress it, hug it
Perhaps you'll hear
The deceased still at your side, earnestly and sincerely exhort you

Don't forget to enjoy the good scenery
When the wind rustles leaves and branches
A flock of birds hopping and singing in the treetop
As if offering greetings

Sunlight, stars and moon provide company
The trees are in touch with each other
As if the memories of the deceased
Linked with each other underground
New and tender shoots sprout contentedly
Each affirming the fruit of cultivation

泊靠在每一棵樹下的魂魄
安息著仍然生長
無論去到了多遠
總會循著原來的路徑
回到親友的懷念裡

Souls moored at the foot of each tree
Resting peacefully, continue to grow
Regardless of how far they go
They'll return by the original road
To the cherished memories of friends and family

2005

汽水

—悼念母親

從急診室
推進手術房之前
你只重複講一句話
我要喝汽水
我們卻遵照醫師囑咐
只是哄著你

從手術房
推入加護病房之後
你持續昏迷
再也沒有機會
喝一口汽水

那最後的要求
是你一輩子
流下多少勞動的汗水
經常口渴
最最卑微的需求
而我們自以為是，不給你

你離去後
日夜如常悄悄輪替
時序如常靜靜推移
我們如常作息
然而悲傷，附生在那一句話
總是一次又一次
讓我們想起你

Soda Pop

—in memory of my mother

Before wheeling you into the operating room
From the emergency ward
You repeatedly said one thing
I want to drink a soda
But we just humored you
As the doctor ordered

After wheeling you into the recovery room
From the operating room
You remained unconscious
And never had another chance
To drink a soda

That final request
Was the humblest of all
For you, who had labored and sweat
Always thirsty
Your whole life
But being bumptious, we denied you

Since you left
Day and night, as always, quietly alternate
The sequence of time, as it always has, quietly elapses
We work and rest as we always have
But the sadness lives on in your words
Always making us think of you
Time after time

2007

橡木桶

圓滾滾的橡木桶
懷藏著濃郁的思念
思念一大片稻田、麥田、果園
彷如詩句醞釀自生活
生活因詩句多了寄託
穀粒、麥粒、果實，發酵為酒香
成為絕美的昇華

農莊村夫
穿過長長細細的田間小路
踏臨酒莊。握鋤的手
學習輕輕晃動酒杯
啜飲琥珀色的醉意

微醺中不時浮現
圓滾滾的橡木桶
循著長長細細的田間小路
回去尋找遼闊的田野
敘舊、傾訴思念

Oak Barrels

Round and roly-poly, the oak barrels
Conceal a longing
Longing for paddy fields, wheat fields, and orchards
Like lines of poetry brewed from life
For poetry is the spiritual sustenance of life
The bouquet of fermented rice, wheat, and fruit
Is the distillation of absolute beauty

A villager from a farm
Threads the long narrow path among the fields
Toward the brewery. His hoe-wielding hands
Have learned to gently tip the wine cup
Sip the intoxicating amber

Amid the tipsiness, the round and roly-poly
Oak barrels frequently appear
He follows the long, narrow field path
In search of vast, open fields
Talking about the old days, pouring out his longings

2010

只能為你寫一首詩

這裡是河川與海洋
相親相愛的交會處
招潮蟹、彈塗魚、大杓鷸、長腳雞
盡情展演的溼地大舞台
白鷺鷥討食的家園
白海豚近海洄游的生命廊道

世代農漁民，在此地
揮灑汗水，享受涼風
迎接潮汐呀！來來去去
泥灘地上形成歷史
稍縱即逝的迷人波紋

這裡的空曠，足夠我們眺望
足夠我們，放開心眼
感受到人生的渺小
以及渺小的樂趣

這裡，是否島嶼後代的子孫
還有機會來到？

名為「國光」的石化工廠
正在逼近，憂傷西海岸
僅存的最後一塊泥灘溼地
名為「建設」的旗幟
正逆著海口的風，大肆揮舞

Writing a Poem Is All I Can Do for You

Here is where river and sea
Meet in loving-kindness
Fiddler crabs, New Guinea mudskippers, far-eastern curlews,
        corn crakes
The wetlands stage where dazzling performances unfold
Home where the egret plucks out its food
The white dolphin's near-shore corridor

On this land, generations of farmers and fishermen
Have wiped away their sweat and enjoyed the cool breeze
Greeting the tides! Ebbing and flowing
History forms on the mudflats
Transient and mesmerizing ripples

The openness permits us a far-off gaze
Enough for us to set our hearts free
To feel the insignificance of life
And the insignificance of interests

Will future generations on this island have
The chance to experience?

A petrochemical plant known as Kuokuang
Is pressuring the anxious and aggrieved west coast
The last remaining mudflats and wetlands
A banner known as 'construction' flutters shamelessly
Against the seaport wind

眼看開發的慾望，預計要
封鎖海岸線，回饋給我們封閉的視野
驅趕美景，回饋給我們煙囪、油污、煙塵瀰漫的天空
眼看少數人的利益
預計要，一路攔截水源
回饋給我們乾旱
眼看沉默的大眾啊，預計要
放任彈塗魚、招潮蟹、長腳雞
放任白鷺鷥與白海豚
甚至放任農漁民死滅
只為了繁榮的口號

這筆帳
環境影響評估
該如何報告

而我只能為你寫一首詩

多麼希望，我的詩句
可以鑄造成子彈
射穿貪得無饜的腦袋
或者冶煉成刀劍
刺入私慾不斷膨脹的胸膛
但我不能。我只能忍抑又忍抑
寫一首哀傷而無用的詩
吞下無比焦慮與悲憤

With the pressure of imminent development, it looks like
The coastline will soon be closed, shutting off our view
The pristine view replaced with smokestacks, oil spills,
         and dust filling the sky
For the benefit of a few
It looks like our water resources will be diverted
With drought as the result for us
It looks like you, the silent masses, will soon vanish
Not to mention the New Guinea mudskipper, fiddler crabs,
         and corn crakes
Not to mention the egrets and white dolphins
And the farmers and fishermen.
All for the slogan of prosperity

How should we report
The environmental impact
Assessment?

And all I can do is write a poem

How I wish my verses
Could be smelted into bullets
Sited into insatiable brains
Or forged into blades
To pierce the expanding breasts of greed
But that's not possible. All I can do is bear it
Writing a sad and useless poem
Swallowing unrivaled worry and sadness

我的詩句不是子彈或刀劍
不能威嚇誰
也不懂得向誰下跪
只有聲聲句句飽含淚水
一遍又一遍朗誦
一遍又一遍，向天地呼喚

My verses are not bullets or blades
They frighten no one
Nor know to whom they should kowtow
They can only fill syllables and lines with tears
One recited after another
One after another, shouting to Heaven and Earth

2010

菜瓜棚

緊接立秋，處暑已過
酷熱仍耍賴不走
不肯隨蟬聲漸歇而退去

整座島嶼密佈的城鎮
每一排樓房每一間
屋子，門窗緊閉
冷氣機全天候呼呼排放
熱騰騰的廢氣
回流給每一條
水泥與柏油牢牢封鎖的街道

我無意和你談論
溫室效應、地球暖化、氣候異常
你已經太熟悉的話題
只想靜靜禮讚
農家庭院、木條竹片
簡易搭起來的菜瓜棚

初春種植的一小株
菜瓜幼苗， 一暝大一寸
敏捷地攀爬蔓延
比巴掌還大片的綠葉
披覆棚架，迎接炎炎夏季
垂下一條一條
清淡自足的菜瓜，與綠蔭

Loofa Arbor

Summer passes, it's nearly autumn
The scorching heat hangs on
Refusing to fade with the cicadas

All the dense cities and towns of the island
Every row of buildings, every
Dwelling, windows and doors sealed tight
Air conditioners running all day long
Blowing hot wasteful air
Flowing back onto every single
Street sealed in asphalt and concrete

I have no intention to speak with you about
The greenhouse effect, global warming, climate change
Topics with which you are all too familiar
All you want to do is praise
The loofa arbor, simply constructed
Of wood and bamboo in the farmer's courtyard

At the beginning of spring, you plated a single
Loofa seedling. Each night it grew one inch
Stretching, climbing quickly
Its leaves larger than the palm of a hand
Covering the arbor, welcoming the summer's scorching days
Hanging down one after another
Mild, self-satisfying gourds in green shade

處暑已過，酷熱仍耍賴不退
我只想在菜瓜棚下
靜靜禮讚，早已被遠遠遺忘的
這一方蔭涼

Summer is nearly over but the scorching heat hangs on
All I want to do under the loofa arbor
Is quietly offer praise for this long forgotten patch
Of cool shade

2011

我心憂懷

你問我平靜近乎安逸的
晚年，還有什麼牽掛
為何滿臉滄桑
每一道皺紋，掩藏不住憂傷

自家庭院樹蔭下
每一陣清風吹拂、每一聲鳥鳴啁啾
都可以作證
我多麼想將滿懷感恩
夾進閒適的詩篇

你問我順遂近乎圓滿的
晚年，還有什麼不足
為何四處奔走
聲嘶力竭地呼喊
每一個腳步，掩飾不住急切

吾鄉遼闊的田野
四時作物歡欣成長、豐饒收成
都可以作證
我多麼想將恬淡知足
譜成歌頌的旋律

我坦然接受年歲老去
而憂傷，點點滴滴
滲進清風、滲進鳥鳴
滲進遼闊的田野
侵蝕著我的閒適與安逸

My Mind Filled with Worries

You ask me in the quiet and ease of my
Later years, what still worries me
Why is my face so troubled
Every wrinkle speaks of worry and sadness

In the shade of the trees in my courtyard
Every cool breeze, all the bird calls
Serve to prove
How much I want to line my poems of leisure and comfort
With the gratitude I feel

You ask me late in a seemingly perfect and satisfying
Life, what is less than satisfying
Why am I constantly on the go running here and there
Shouting stridently
Every footstep fails to hide my impatience

The broad fields of my village
Vigorous crops all year round and bountiful harvests
All serve to prove
How much I wish to compose the melodies
Of my songs with quiet satisfaction

I calmly accept the sadness of
Aging, every tiny bit and drop
Permeated with the cool breeze and bird calls
Permeated with the broad fields of my village
Eating away at my leisure and comfort

我確實經常滿懷憂傷
憂傷阻擋不住
挾開發為名的洪流，繼續氾濫
掠奪了山林、掠奪河川
掠奪了田地、掠奪海岸
一地又一地，抵押舉債
佔領，糟蹋殆盡，而後
毀棄，留下萬劫不復

我確實經常滿懷
憂傷，看望未來
總有一天
越滾越龐大的環境債務
勢將背負不起
宣告徹底破產
哪裡還有安身立命之處

In fact my mind is always filled with worry
I can't stop worrying
Held hostage by a torrent called development
          that continues to spread far and wide
Pillaging the mountain forests, plundering the rivers
Pillaging the fields, plundering the coast
One piece of land after another, mortgaged off
Occupied, degraded, and later
Totally ruined, never to be restored

Truly, my mind is always filled
With worries, looking at the future
The cost to the environment will grow so enormous
No one will be able to bear
And absolute bankruptcy will be declared
Then where will peace and stability be found?

2011

春氣始至

春氣始至、四時之始
立春悄悄降臨
雨水緊跟著依約而來
綿綿密密灑落
島嶼平原，新翻耕的田土
忙碌吸吮

溫柔雨聲懇切邀請你
貼近遼闊田野
貼近新式有機栽培農園
傾聽每一粒種子在萌芽
每一株幼苗在抽長
如何回報雨水的疼惜

驚蟄日、雷鳴動
水稻、蔬菜與瓜果
翠綠伸展的枝葉
欣欣然迎接春分、清明、穀雨 ……
更豐沛的雨水

不論時代潮流怎樣翻滾
我只確定，沒有任何人、任何數字
可以估算清風、估算春雨
估算一季又一季豐饒的收成
估算世世代代
平靜的安身立命
有多少經濟產值

Burgeoning Spring

Spring burgeons, the start of the four seasons
The Beginning of Spring quietly arrives
The rain, as promised, follows close behind
Sprinkling continuously
The flatlands of the island, the newly turned soil
Busily absorbs

The gentle sound of rain invites you sincerely
To press close to the broad fields
To press close to the new-style organic farm
To listen as each seed sprouts
As each seedling grows
Repaying the rain's kindness

During the period of Waking Insects, thunder rumbles, shaking
The rice, vegetables, melons and fruit
The green leaves and stems stretch out joyfully
To welcome the Vernal Equinox, Pure Brightness,
                    and Grain Rain . . .
And even more copious amounts of rain

Despite how the trends of the age roll on
I'm certain no one, no set number
Can calculate the cool breeze, calculate the spring rain
Calculate the abundant harvest from one season to the next
Calculate the economic value of the output
Of settling down and getting on with life's work
Generation after generation

2011

大雪無雪

接連幾陣陰雨
悄悄降下立冬

立冬之後，小雪無雪
大雪，也無雪；在島嶼平原
姹紫嫣紅遍佈田野
翠綠作物依然豐饒
只有幾波冷氣團
加深些許冬意

雪，在高山峻嶺
如細碎、潔白的花瓣
紛飛飄落，白茫茫覆蓋峰頂
吸引大批賞雪人潮

二十四節氣，走在農民曆裡
亞熱帶島嶼，自有獨特的季候
時而南方熱氣壓上揚
時而北方寒流來襲
忽熱忽冷，如生命無常多變

小寒、大寒，歲暮蕭條
預告春氣又將至
漫漫寒夜引領我們，沉靜思慮
天與地，如何依時循環

No Snow in the Time of Great Snow

After several bouts of overcast and rain
The Beginning of Winter quietly arrives

After the Beginning of Winter, no snow in the time of Lesser Snow
Nor any snow in the time of Great Snow, on the island's flatlands
The fields are beautiful and luxuriant
Green crops as abundant as ever
Just a few masses of cold air
Make it feel a bit more like winter

Snow on the mountain peaks
Like brittle, pure-white petals
Flakes fly and fall, covering the peaks in white
Attracting great numbers to enjoy

The twenty-four solar terms and their procession through the
farmer's almanac
A subtropical island has its own climate and seasons
Sometimes hot pressure rises from the south
Sometimes a cold current flows from the north
Now hot, now cold, transient and changeable as life

Lesser Cold, Great Cold, the desolate end of the year
Predict the coming of spring
The long, cold night makes us think of
How Heaven and Earth comply with the cycle of time

2013

一起回來呀

—為農鄉水田濕地復育計畫而作

向天敬拜
向地彎身
向歷代祖先，訴說感念
濁水溪平原遼闊
賜與我們，日日
和黑色土壤殷勤打交道
承續做農的行業

每一株作物都體現
我們溫柔的深情
見證我們強韌的意志
任寒氣、烈日，輪流試煉
任經濟的風潮
席捲過一遍又一遍

深深懷念起
水草搖擺、青蛙跳躍
魚蝦螃蟹漫游嬉戲
泥鰍翻攪泥巴
蚯蚓在地底鑽動
水蛇草蛇悠哉出沒
蜜蜂、蜻蜓、蝙蝠、螢火蟲……
飛鳥，從並不遙遠的過去
展翅飛了回來
穿越險阻的呼喚
回來呀，回來
一起回來呀

Come Back Together

—for the paddy field and wetlands restoration plan

Bow to Heaven
Bow to Earth
Express gratitude to our ancestors
For bestowing on us
The broad Zhuoshui River plain,
Every day we are attentive in our contact with the black soil
Continuing the profession of farming

Every crop embodies
Our gentle love
Testifies to our strong will
Let the cold air and scorching sun temper us in turn
Let economic volatility
Take away everything, one after another

Thinking fondly of
The swaying grass, jumping frogs
The pleasant playing and roaming of fish, crabs, and shrimp
Loaches turning in the mud
Earthworms burrowing in the soil
The carefree comings and goings of water snakes, grass snakes
Bees, dragonflies, bats, and fireflies. . . .
Flying birds from the not too distant past
Return on spread wings
Passing through dangers, calling out
O, come back, come back
Come back together

我們凝神傾聽
水田蕩漾的記憶
重新學習友善土地
彼此約束，相互打氣
（守護灌溉水源
拒絕使用化學藥劑）
耐心等待消失的
會再豐富回來

我們懷抱希望
向風伸展
向水找尋
向世間萬物證明
堅守，做農的價值
創造家園的美好
看顧島嶼的糧倉
是多麼榮耀

We listen intently to the
Undulating memories of the paddy field
Learning again from the good earth
Bound together, mutually supportive
(Protecting irrigation water
Rejecting the use of chemicals)
Patiently awaiting the return
Of vanished abundance

Our cherished hope
Spreads to the wind
Searches the waters
Proves to all in the world that
Holding fast to farming's values
Creating a home of beauty
Looking after the island's granary
Is the greatest honor

2014